A Gift For

→ FROM ←

Mars and Venus
The Languages of Love

JOHN GRAY, Ph.D.

THE BEST OF MARS AND VENUS COMPILED EXCLUSIVELY FOR HALLMARK

BOOKS

HarperCollins*Publishers*

BOK4008

Published under license from HarperCollins Publishers, Inc.

ISBN 0-06-095397-7

00 01 02 03 RRD 10 9 8 7 6 5

Contents

Mars and Venus

The Languages of Love

1

Men Are from Mars, Women Are from Venus

*I*magine that men are from Mars and women are from Venus. One day long ago the Martians, looking through their telescopes, discovered the Venusians. Just glimpsing the Venusians awakened feelings they had never known. They fell in love and quickly invented space travel and flew to Venus.

The Venusians welcomed the Martians with open arms. They had intuitively known that this day would come. Their hearts opened wide to a love they had never felt before.

The love between the Venusians and Martians was magical. They delighted in being together, doing things together, and sharing together. Though from different worlds, they reveled in their differences. They spent months learning about each other, exploring and appreciating their different needs, preferences, and behavior patterns. For years they lived together in love and harmony.

Then they decided to fly to Earth. In the beginning everything was wonderful and beautiful. But the effects of Earth's atmosphere took hold, and one morning everyone woke up with a peculiar kind of amnesia—*selective amnesia*!

Both the Martians and Venusians forgot that they were from different planets and were supposed to be different. In one morning everything they had learned about their differences was erased from their memory. And since that day men and women have been in conflict.

Remembering Our Differences

Without the awareness that we are supposed to be different, men and women are at odds with each other. We usually become angry or frustrated with the opposite sex because we have forgotten this important truth. We expect the opposite sex to be more like ourselves. We desire them to "want what we want" and "feel the way we feel."

We mistakenly assume that if our partners love us they will react and behave in certain ways—the ways we react and behave when we love someone. This attitude sets us up to be disappointed again and again and prevents us from taking the necessary time to communicate lovingly about our differences.

> **We mistakenly assume that if our partners love us they will react and behave in certain ways—the ways we react and behave when we love someone.**

Men mistakenly expect women to think, communicate, and react the way men do; women mistakenly expect men to feel, communicate, and respond the way women do. We have forgotten that men and women are supposed to be different. As a result our relationships are filled with unnecessary friction and conflict.

Clearly recognizing and respecting these differences dramatically reduce confusion when dealing with the opposite sex. When you remember that men are from Mars and women are from Venus, everything can be explained.

An Overview of Our Differences

Throughout this book I will discuss in great detail our differences. Each chapter will bring you new and crucial insights. Here are the major differences that we will explore:

We will look at how men's and women's values are inherently different and try to understand the two biggest mistakes we make in relating to the opposite sex: men mistakenly offer solutions and invalidate feelings while women offer unsolicited advice and direction. Through understanding our Martian/Venusian backgrounds it becomes obvious why men and women *unknowingly* make these mistakes. By remembering these differences we can correct our mistakes and immediately respond to each other in more productive ways.

Here, we'll discover the different ways men and women cope with stress. While Martians tend to pull away and silently think about what's bothering them, Venusians feel an instinctive need to talk about what's bothering them. You will learn new strategies for getting what you want at these conflicting times.

We will then explore how to motivate the opposite sex. Men are motivated when they feel needed, while women are motivated when they feel cherished. We will discuss the steps for improving relationships and explore how to overcome our greatest challenges: men need to overcome their resistance to giving love while women must overcome their resistance to receiving it.

You'll also learn how men and women commonly misunderstand each other because they speak different languages. A *Martian/ Venusian Phrase Dictionary* is provided to translate commonly misunderstood expressions. You will learn how men and women speak and even stop speaking for entirely different reasons. Women will learn what to do when a man stops talking, and men will learn how to listen better without becoming frustrated.

We will discover how men and women have different needs for intimacy. A man gets close but then inevitably needs to pull away. Women will learn how to support this pulling-away process so he will spring back to her like a rubber band. Women also will learn the best times for having intimate conversations with a man.

You'll discover how men and women give the kind of love they need and not what the opposite sex needs. Men primarily need a kind of love that is trusting, accepting, and appreciative. Women primarily need a kind of love that is caring, understanding, and respectful. You will also discover the most common ways you may unknowingly be turning off your partner.

We will explore how to avoid painful arguments. Men will learn that by acting as if they are always right they may invalidate a woman's feelings. Women will learn how they unknowingly send messages of disapproval instead of disagreement, thus igniting a man's defenses.

You'll also learn ways to communicate with each other during difficult times. The different ways men and women hide feelings are discussed along with the importance of sharing feelings.

You will understand why Venusians have a more difficult time asking for support, as well as why Martians commonly resist requests. You will learn the secrets for encouraging a man to give more and discover in various ways the power of being brief, direct, and using the correct wording.

In each chapter of this book, you will discover new secrets for creating loving and lasting relationships. Each new discovery will increase your ability to have fulfilling relationships.

Good Intentions Are Not Enough

Falling in love is always magical. It feels eternal, as if love will last forever. We naïvely believe that somehow we are exempt from the problems our parents had, free from the odds that love will die, assured that it is meant to be and that we are destined to live happily ever after.

But as the magic recedes and daily life takes over, it emerges that men continue to expect women to think and react like men, and women expect men to feel and behave like women. Without a clear awareness of our differences, we do not take the time to understand and respect each other. We become demanding, resentful, judgmental, and intolerant.

With the best and most loving intentions love continues to die. Somehow the problems creep in. The resentments build. Communication breaks down. Mistrust increases. Rejection and repression result. The magic of love is lost.

We ask ourselves:

How does it happen?

Why does it happen?

Why does it happen to us?

To answer these questions our greatest minds have developed brilliant and complex philosophical and psychological models. Yet still the old patterns return. Love dies. It happens to almost everyone.

Each day millions of individuals are searching for a partner to experience that special loving feeling. Each year, millions of couples join together in love and then painfully separate because they have lost that loving feeling. From those who are able to sustain love long enough to get married, only 50 percent stay married. Out of those who stay together, possibly another 50 percent are not fulfilled. They stay together out of loyalty and obligation or from the fear of starting over.

Very few people, indeed, are able to grow in love. Yet, it does happen. When men and women are able to respect and accept their differences then love has a chance to blossom.

> **When men and women are able
> to respect and accept their differences
> then love has a chance to blossom.**

Through understanding the hidden differences of the opposite sex we can more successfully give and receive the love that is in our hearts. By validating and accepting our differences, creative solutions can be discovered whereby we can succeed in getting what we want. And, more important, we can learn how to best love and support the people we care about.

Love is magical, and it can last, if we remember our differences.

2

A New Job Description for Relationships

*T*he reason there are so many problems in relationships today is that we just don't understand each other. Men, in particular, don't understand what women need to be happy, and women don't know how to communicate their needs in a language that men understand. Old relationship skills are no longer effective, and are many times counterproductive. With an updated understanding of modern pressures and needs we can begin to formulate a new job description for relationships that can nurture and support both men and women.

Old relationship skills required men to be effective providers and protectors while women learned to be pleasing and accommodating. If strictly observed today, these old skills would go from being the solution to being the problem. When modern men focus on being better providers and protectors, they only burn out, working more and spending less time sharing in their relationships.

Let's look at a playful example of how times have changed. When men were hunters, it was much easier to have relationships. It used to be fine if a man was late getting home. When he eventually did return home, his wife was happy that he was still alive.

The harder and longer he worked, the more she felt taken care of. Now, when he is late it is taken as a sign that he doesn't care, and he is in the doghouse. Our fathers had a much easier time in their relationships; not only were they not rejected but they didn't even have to remember to call home.

On the other hand, women didn't mind being pleasing and accommodating to a man when he came home because he was generally very tired and went to sleep. Now, with men spending more time at home, women begin to feel as if they give more than they are getting in return. From this playful perspective, our mothers seem to have had it much easier when men spent more time away from home.

When modern women focus on being more pleasing and accommodating, they end up feeling like martyrs who sacrifice their own needs to ensure harmony in the relationship. For women, practicing old relationship skills today is like setting a time bomb. They gradually become so overworked that they explode, feeling resentful, overwhelmed, and unsupported. Although they love their partners, it is hard to *be* loving. Men, seeing that their mates are not happy, assume that they have failed as providers and, in time, withdraw completely.

The only antidote to despair and divorce is the application of new relationship skills based on new job descriptions for both men and women.

Our Parents Never Told Us It Would Be Like This

If a woman is unwaveringly pleasing and accommodating according to the old ways, her man will never get the message that she needs a different kind of support. A man generally doesn't have a clue as to what a woman really needs on an emotional level. He is too busy feeling the pressure to be a better provider. When a woman complains, he hears it simply as her wanting more, which implies that he isn't giving enough. Not knowing what to do, he will just withdraw. Feeling unappreciated, a man who uses old relationship skills commonly reacts by doing less. He figures that if this isn't enough, then why bother trying to do more.

New relationship skills are imperative for women today to get what they need from men.

No wonder so many contemporary women feel so hopeless about men.

In previous generations, women could focus on being pleasing, accommodating, and nondemanding because men were well trained and knew their jobs. Women didn't need to ask for help or learn how to communicate their wishes to men because men received a clear job description from their fathers and their culture. A woman did not need to instruct her partner; instead she could focus on appreciating his efforts and forgiving his mistakes.

Doing Less but Supporting More

When a woman shares her frustrations of the day, a man hears her wanting him to solve all her problems. For men, the thought of having to do more is many times a strong message that they are not doing enough. Feeling unappreciated, it is difficult for men to find the energy and motivation to do more.

When a man hears that he is not required to solve her problems or do more in the home, but is primarily needed to listen when she wants to talk and be supported emotionally, then when she talks he can relax and begin to really listen.

When a woman gives a man the message that he can do less and support more by listening, he will slowly but surely begin to have more energy and will automatically begin offering to help out. When a man truly understands a problem, an inner energy then emerges to assist him in solving it. When he is told he is the problem and must do more, he feels little energy and is very resistant.

While women want men to do more, men want to feel that they are doing enough. The most successful approach in a relationship is to focus first on creating good communication, where a man can feel appreciated for being empathetic, sympathetic, and understanding. As he begins to listen more and is appreciated for supporting her in this way, he will almost magically begin to do more.

To get what they need from their men, women must learn how to communicate needs and desires without demanding or finger-pointing. In most cases, as we will discover, a woman can be made happier by a man who is actually doing less because he is supporting her differently, according to new rules which are infinitely more effective. When a man understands this truth, his motivation to do things differently greatly increases.

Part of a man's frustration is that when a woman wants more he mistakenly assumes that he has to do everything she needs. He does not know that as long as he is taking small steps toward helping her around the house, coupled with better communication, she will be immeasurably happier.

As both partners begin successfully to give and receive the support they really need, they will happily give increasingly more. He will give her more of what modern women most need and appreciate. She will give him more of what men really want.

> **Today, we can detect a definite generational shift away from rigidly defined gender job roles and toward wholeness.**

To discover the behavior patterns that nourish femininity and masculinity, let's return for a moment to the world of the male provider and his nurturer mate. Religion and social convention encouraged differences between men and women, particularly through assigning specific roles. This division of labor held steady for millennia, well into our parents' time.

The hunter's day was filled with risk and danger and was primarily focused on the single task of successfully protecting the home and bringing home the kill. The life of his family depended on his competence, assertiveness, aggressiveness, and skill. Men evolved in specific ways to cope successfully with the pressures of "men's work."

A nurturer's day was a flow of repetitive and detailed tasks that sustained her children, her family, and her community. The life of her family depended on her ability to communicate, negotiate, accommodate, and cooperate. Women also evolved in specific ways to cope successfully with the stresses of "women's work."

Today, the lines dividing men's work and women's work are dramatically fading. This shift away from rigidly defined gender roles provides greater freedom, but it also generates new stress. With a greater understanding and respect for how our ancestors coped with stress, we can be better equipped to support each other during this transformation.

How Our Ancestors Coped

On a very basic level, our brains and bodies have, over the millennia, developed specifically to deal with the unique stresses of traditional men's and women's work. Although modern lifestyles are rapidly dispensing with those roles, evolution has yet to catch up and produce new coping mechanisms.

Chief among the traditional female coping mechanisms is communication. For the nurturer women of long ago, talking in a non-goal-oriented way, while giving and receiving sympathy, was essential to peace of mind and generated feelings of security and belonging. Years ago, women with children were much more vulnerable and were dependent on the goodwill of others. Before government welfare programs and expanded legal rights and educational opportunities, women had to rely on others for security and safety. If her husband left her or died, a woman depended on her family and community to take care of her, so she had to maintain strong relationships with those around her. Talking connected her to her support network and made her feel secure. When a modern woman today is upset and begins talking, she is automatically connecting with that time-honored feeling of security.

Why Women Need to Talk About Problems

As a common practice, nurturer women shared their problems with each other not directly to ask for help but to share sympathy and community. Problem solving was secondary to the exercise of the cooperative spirit.

Women supported each other unconditionally, without being asked and expecting nothing in return. This cooperative sharing strengthened relationships within the community and ensured a woman's and her children's survival should she be widowed.

Talking about problems, sharing feelings, and articulating desires became a feminine ritual to create greater intimacy and express loyalty to the community. Today, when a woman goes to a counselor, she is seeking out that same support. Most counselors and therapists, it should be noted, are trained to listen attentively rather than focus on problem solving. Hence, the process offers tremendous support for women in coping with day-to-day stress.

Through talking and feeling heard in therapy, women come to feel nurtured, and the weight of their problems lifts. Once able to relax and proceed at a more easygoing pace, they can begin to deal with their problems.

When Men Offer Advice

Men instinctively don't understand this and, unlike therapists, are not trained in how to support feelings effectively. When a woman talks about her feelings, he assumes she is seeking his help to solve her problems and instinctively responds to her feelings by offering help or advice.

Take a fireman, for example. When he receives a call, he must get the size and location of the fire as quickly as possible and then do something to put out the fire. Asking a lot of extra questions and offering empathy is not part of his job description.

Imagine this scene. A fireman receives a call and responds by saying, "You have a fire. How awful. How does it feel? Really." Obviously, this kind of empathetic response would be out of place.

When a man becomes restless while listening to a woman it is not because he doesn't care about her. It's because every cell in his body is saying: If there is a fire, let's get out of here and put it out. If there is a problem, he wants to do something about it and not just talk about it.

Modern men need to understand that modern women need, more than anything else, the opportunity to talk about their feelings without focusing on solving the problems that cause them. By responding with empathy, sympathy, and understanding, he makes sure that her female side is nurtured so that she can throw off her feelings of being overwhelmed.

> **In a practical sense, by just listening a man frees
> a woman to forget the urgency of her problems
> and remember what a great guy he is.**

When a woman is unhappy and talks about problems, a man must remind himself that it is not him but modern culture that demands she must bear the stress of having two full-time careers—homemaker and wage earner—at once. Remembering that he is not the prime source of her frustration helps him to not feel blamed when she is unhappy. This awareness frees him to sympathize with her rather than defend himself.

How Men Cope

Men commonly cope with stress differently. For instance, by working at achieving a simple goal like driving the car, or hitting a tennis ball around, teeing off, or shooting hoops, a man sorts out his thoughts and concerns, clarifies his values and priorities, and develops a plan of action. It gives him a sense of security.

Remember, a hunter's survival is ensured by moving quietly and then striking. Through his hunting—or problem-solving—skills, his family's security is ensured. It is the subconscious hunter, buried deep inside the contemporary man, who feels secure when he lobs a paper ball into the wastebasket across the room.

If a man can put his feelings into action, he begins to feel more in control. By simply pacing back and forth when he is frustrated, he can find the same relief a woman might feel through talking. Through understanding this vital difference, men and women can more effectively support each other.

Silently Sitting on a Rock

Traditionally, men have dealt with their problems by silently and patiently thinking up solutions. Ancient hunters would sit on a rock and silently search the horizon, looking and listening for their prey, or looking across the plains at their target, studying its movements and planning the attack.

This process of sitting, waiting, scheming, and planning allowed him to relax and conserve energy for the inevitable chase. Focusing on the solution kept his mind off the fear of being attacked or of missing his target, and when he achieved his goal he returned home a happy, stress-free man.

> Women cope with stress through sharing in nurturing relationships, men by solving problems.

Why Men Watch TV

When a modern man comes home, quite commonly he sits in his favorite chair and either reads the newspaper or watches TV. Like the ancient hunter who needed to recover from the stress of his day, he instinctively finds his rock to sit on and begins gazing off into the horizon.

Through reading or listening to the news he is, in effect, looking out over the world or scanning the horizon. As he picks up the remote control and begins searching through the stations, or turns the pages of his paper, he is once more in control: he silently and swiftly continues his hunt.

As he assumes this ancient posture, he becomes more comfortable. Feelings of security automatically begin to emerge. Feeling in control, he is able to most effectively cope with the stress of not having immediate solutions to the problems of his life.

Through this instinctive ritual he is able temporarily to forget his problems at work and is eventually ready for the relationship.

When Women Don't Understand Men

When men today attempt to fulfill their need to be solitary, the modern woman commonly misunderstands. She mistakenly assumes that he wants her to initiate a conversation. She thinks he is waiting for her to notice that he is distressed, and that he wants her to ask him what is bothering him. She does not realize that he really wants to be left alone.

When she persists in asking, he becomes increasingly annoyed and sends her what he thinks are clear messages to leave him alone, but she misinterprets his cues. Here is a common pattern.

She Says:	He Says:
1. *She says:* "How was your day?"	1. *He says:* "Fine."
She means: "Let's talk, I'm interested in your day, and I hope you are interested in mine."	He means: "I am giving you a short answer because I need some time alone."
2. *She says:* "How did your meeting go with your new client?"	2. *He says:* "It was OK."
She means: "I will keep asking you questions so you know that I really care and I am interested in your day. I hope you will be interested in my day. I have a lot to say."	He means: "I am trying to be polite and not reject you, but would you stop bothering me with more questions?"

She Says:	He Says:
3. *She says:* "Did they like your proposal?" She means: "I suppose it must be hard to talk about it, so I'll ask a more neutral question to get us started. It's OK if you don't open up right away. I am here for you, and I am interested. I know you will really appreciate it, and then you will want to hear what I have to say."	3. *He says:* "Yes." He means: "Look, I don't want to talk right now. Would you just leave me alone? You're bugging me. Can't you tell I want to be alone? If I wanted to talk I would talk."
4. *She says:* "What's wrong?" She means: "I can see that something happened that is upsetting you. You can talk to me. I will listen, I care. I'm sure that by talking about it you will feel better."	4. *He says:* "Nothing's wrong." He means: "Nothing's wrong that I can't deal with alone. After a while I will forget my problems and then be available for the relationship. So would you just ignore me for a little while and then I will be much more open and interested in you. I just need to shift gears to get back home."
5. *She says:* "I can tell something is wrong. What is it?" She means: "I know something is wrong, and if you don't talk, it will get worse. You need to talk!"	5. *He says nothing and walks away.* He means: "I don't want to get mad at you, so I am just walking away. After a while I will be back, and I will not be mad at you for annoying me."

How Women React When Men Don't Want to Talk

Inevitably, when a man resists conversation and a woman doesn't understand his need to be alone to recuperate from the day, she will have a variety of misinterpretations and begin to panic. These are some of the ways in which she may then react:

She Thinks:	She Reacts:
1. She thinks there is some big problem in the relationship and he doesn't want to be with her.	1. She reacts by feeling rejected, and to clear things up insists on discussing their relationship.
2. She thinks he doesn't trust her to care about his feelings.	2. She reacts sympathetically by asking lots of questions and trying to show that she cares. Eventually, she feels frustrated when he resists her loving attempts to help.
3. She thinks he must be angry with her.	3. She reacts by feeling inadequate and confused.
4. She thinks he doesn't want to talk because he is hiding something that might upset her.	4. As a result, she does get upset worrying about what it might be.
5. She thinks he is selfish and only cares about himself and not about her.	5. In reaction, she doubts his love for her.
6. She thinks he is trying to punish her by withholding his love and attention.	6. She reacts by getting angry back and withholding her attention and love.

She Thinks:	She Reacts:
7. She thinks he is dissatisfied with her.	7. She reacts by feeling unappreciated for all she does for him.
8. She thinks he is just lazy.	8. In reaction, she feels resentful because she is giving so much more than he is.
9. She thinks he has lost interest in her.	9. She reacts by feeling ignored, isolated, and powerless to get what she needs. She may also begin to feel unattractive, boring, and unworthy of love.
10. She thinks he has a deep fear of intimacy brought about by his dysfunctional past and that he needs therapy.	10. She reacts by feeling powerless to ever get what she needs until he is healed.
11. She thinks he is hiding something from her.	11. She reacts by feeling afraid that she has done something bad or that he has done something bad.
12. She thinks she got involved with the wrong man.	12. She reacts by thinking other men are not this way and longs for a more sensitive and talkative man.

In each of these examples, the woman's reaction is based on a misunderstanding. If a woman is to support a man in coming back to the relationship, her new job description requires her to understand this difference and accept his need for space. As we will continue to see, this doesn't mean that she must sacrifice her need for conversation. What is required, however, is a new sense of timing.

Why Men Pull Away

When a woman learns the skill of temporarily postponing her needs and allows a man the time he needs to shift gears from his work life to his home life, she creates a fertile ground for him to find his love for her and then act on it. As he grows accustomed to this support, he begins to anticipate it. At this point, just the thought of returning home begins releasing his stress. The more he gets this kind of support, the less he needs to pull away from his mate.

Without this new relationship skill a woman unknowingly prevents her male partner from successfully making the transition from work to home. Through her demanding more of him or reacting negatively to his need for private time, he may never relax enough to come back into the relationship. If the downward spiral continues, it can actually hinder a man from contacting his loving feelings. He may even believe that he doesn't love his partner anymore.

> **When a man arrives home to a needy woman,
> he continues to pull away.**

The more he feels pressured to talk or be "in relationship," the more he needs to back off to relax. He can most effectively forget the demands of his job when he feels no pressure or demands from his mate.

When a man returns home to a nondemanding woman, he feels free to take the time he needs to relax. He can then automatically shift gears and give his partner the love she deserves.

Literally thousands of women who have applied this relationship skill report that this single insight has magically transformed their relationships.

....
When a man is not expected to give more, he automatically wants to.
....

When Men Don't Understand Women

When a woman is emotionally distressed, a man mistakenly assumes that if she is to feel better, she needs some solitary time just as he does. He will tend to ignore her and give her lots of space because that is precisely the kind of support he would want. To ignore her, though, is the worst thing he can do.

Even if he asks her what is bothering her, he may misread what she really needs. Again, let's look at a common pattern.

Tom says to Mary, "What's wrong? You seem upset."

Mary says, "Oh, it's nothing." Mary is silently saying, "Nothing is bothering me, unless of course you really care. Then you will show me by standing here and asking me more questions."

Tom says, "OK," and walks away. He is silently saying, "It's OK if you don't want to talk about it. I understand if you want some space. I'll support you by acting like everything is OK. I trust that you can handle it."

Tom actually thinks he is being supportive and has no idea that he has just failed the test. Most men think like Tom, but almost any woman would instinctively understand that when Mary said, "Nothing's wrong," she really wanted him to ask more questions and draw her out. When a woman says "Nothing's wrong," something usually is, and she needs to talk about it to a listener who is interested and cares. She wants to be asked questions that will eventually help her to open up.

Let's look at some other common ways in which men misunderstand women.

1. He asks: "Do you want to talk about something?"	1. She says "No" but really means "Yes, and if you really care, you will ask more questions."
2. He asks: "Do you want any help?"	2. She says "No, I can do it" but really means "Yes, and if you really want to help, then watch what I am doing and join in."
3. He asks: "Did I do something wrong?"	3. She says "No" but really means "Yes, and if you care to make things better you will figure out what by asking more questions."
4. He asks: "Is everything OK?"	4. She says "Yes" but really means "No, and if you want to work it out, then you will ask more questions about what might be upsetting me."

In each of these examples, the woman is testing to see if it is safe to talk about her feelings. If he understands her hidden meaning, then she is assured that she can share her feelings and that her needs will be supported.

Without a clear job description of what he is supposed to do at such times, few men have a clue and just walk away thinking they are being helpful.

When Women Talk About Feelings

After feeling neglected for some time, when a woman does eventually talk about her feelings a man will again misunderstand. Commonly, he misinterprets her complaints and assumes that he is required to be a better provider instead of hearing that she really needs more attention and nurturing at home. Let's look at some common examples.

She Complains:	He Misunderstands:
1. When she complains about the house, she is really only wanting to share her frustrations and be heard.	1. He thinks that he has to earn more money for a bigger house before she will be happy.
2. When she complains about her job, she is really only wanting to share her day and reconnect with her partner.	2. He thinks that he has to make more money so that she doesn't have to work, and only then will she be happy.
3. When she complains about having to do housework, she is generally sharing her feelings of being overwhelmed and is asking for help if he has the energy.	3. He thinks that he has to either provide a maid or become one for her, and only then will she be happy.
4. When she complains about the weather or other problems with no solution, she is generally seeking a little sympathy for what she has been through.	4. Emotionally, he begins to feel as if he has to earn more money so that they can move to a better climate before she will be happy.

She Complains:	He Misunderstands:
5. When she complains that he works too hard, she is wanting him to know that she misses him and would love to spend more time together.	5. He thinks that he now has to make more money so that he doesn't have to work so hard, and then she will be happy.

In every case, when the woman is distressed the man feels on a deep instinctual level that he has to work harder to be a better provider. This instinct to succeed more at work causes him to be less present in the relationship. When he does become more successful, or when he does exert himself to solve her problems and she is still unhappy or unfulfilled, he feels ever more intensely the frustration of not being able to make her happy. To cope with this frustration he begins to turn off his romantic feelings of caring about her fulfillment.

Why Men Don't Commit

This same principle applies to many single men. When they don't attract the woman of their dreams, they begin to feel as if they have to make more money. Instead of recognizing that they need to work on relationship skills, they may focus too much on their careers.

Some men give up on the thought of marriage because their particular talents make it seem unlikely that they will earn big money, or they feel that they'll have to sacrifice themselves too much to make a large salary. Some men may have the woman of their dreams but are afraid to commit because they don't make enough money.

Jackie and Dan are a very dramatic example of this. They had been living together for nine years. She wanted to get married, but he didn't. He assured her that he loved her, but something inside was stopping him from getting married. He claimed that he just wasn't sure. Then, one evening while talking about a movie they had seen, she happened to say, "I'd love you even if we were always poor."

The very next day, he went out and bought the ring.

All Dan needed was a clear message from Jackie that he didn't have to make a lot of money to successfully provide for her happiness. Then he could make the commitment. Like most men, Dan was able to commit to the relationship when he felt his ability to provide for a woman was enough to make her happy.

While all men are not as obsessed with making money, they do need to feel confident that they can provide for a woman's happiness before making a commitment to marriage. New relationship skills help a man realize that, regardless of how much money he makes, he can provide emotional support and a woman will be much happier.

Why Men Become Preoccupied with Work

When a man experiences the stress of thinking that his family is unhappy, he instinctively focuses more and more on succeeding at work. He focuses to such an extent that he doesn't realize how much time he is away. For him, time may pass very quickly, but while she is waiting for him to come home it passes much more slowly. He doesn't realize that in modern times, his presence at home is at least as important to her as his success at work.

The more work stress a man experiences, the more he focuses on solving problems. At such times it is extremely difficult for him to release his lock on the problem and bring his full attention back to relationships. He can become so focused that he forgets everything else and unknowingly neglects his wife and family.

It is as though he is looking through a tunnel and only takes in what is relevant or useful to achieving his goal. He doesn't realize that he is not listening or responding to the people he loves because he is so utterly focused on solving his problem. At such times, he has temporarily forgotten what is really important to him. He does not recognize that he is pushing away the people he loves the most.

When a Man Ignores His Family

When a man withdraws from intimacy to focus on his work problems, it is hard for a woman to recognize it as an automatic reaction. She views it as a deliberate act of coldness and indifference because for a woman to focus on work issues and ignore her family would require a deliberate decision on her part and, in most cases, would also signal that she just doesn't care.

When a man is focused on his work, he doesn't just decide to ignore his family. He truly forgets. He doesn't decide to forget picking up his daughter at school, it is an automatic by-product of increasing his focus on solving his problems at work. It is not a sign that he has stopped caring. If anything, it is a sign that he does care but is just not adept at coping with his stress.

This same tendency to focus on one thing and forget everything else causes a man to procrastinate about doing things he really is willing to do. Many times a woman will ask a man to do something he really intends to do, but then he forgets. Since it is actually hard for her to forget, she makes the mistake of assuming that he is deliberately trying to get out of a chore by putting it off.

A man today cannot simply make a kill as his ancestors did and then come home to celebrate. His life is much more complex. It may take months to finish a deal and make a killing. During that time his mind is consumed. He thinks at work, at home, and in his sleep. He can remember every detail required to achieve his work goals, but he then forgets to bring home the milk no matter how many times his wife reminds him.

Shifting Gears from Work to the Relationship

A man's tendency to be absorbed in his work not only is counter-productive for a woman, but it is also counterproductive for him. Until a man can apply new relationship skills and directly nurture a woman's feelings, his instincts will urge him back to his work when she is upset or unfulfilled.

There are basically three ways in which a man is able to shift gears between work and the relationship. To various degrees, all three are simultaneously required.

I. Success

The more successful a man feels when he leaves work, the easier it is for him to forget his problems and enjoy his relationships. A successful day at work makes him feel that the hunt is over and he can now return home and more easily relax. When a man is not succeeding as much as he would like, or as much as he thinks he should, then the next two ways become more important.

2. Distraction

To forget the problems of his day, he distracts his focus from work to sitting on his favorite rock and watching TV, reading the paper, listening to music, going to the movies, or any other easy and non-demanding activities requiring focus.

Another practical way for him to shift gears through distraction is to work out, focusing his mind on exercising his body. This can be vigorous activity or even something as easy as going for a walk. To free his mind from solving problems at work, he just needs a new challenge that requires focus.

A man forgets his real problems by focusing on other problems he can easily solve or problems he is not responsible for solving. Playing games, fiddling or tinkering with things, cheering on teams, playing sports, and watching the news are the most common stress reducers. When he mentally solves the world's problems or figures out how to get his team to win, he feels competent again and confident about facing his real-life problems.

> **Without a hobby, a man may not be able to
> disengage himself from work and
> can become overstressed.**

Indulging in a hobby allows him to forget the really pressing and important problems.

To encourage or expect a man to be in his female side and talk about his problems in many cases goes against his nature. In some cases, talking about his day before he is relaxed may increase his stress by bringing his awareness back to work, with all its frustrations, disappointments, and worries.

First, a man needs to forget his problems and then he feels as if he has something positive to offer. He will then automatically remember what is most important to him—his wife and family or the desire to have one. This shift in awareness to what is really important to him is also essential for him to recharge.

3. Appreciation

The third means to shift gears from work to the relationship is to return home anticipating the support of his partner. A woman's accepting and appreciating love is something he begins to look forward to. To anticipate this support makes him feel that he is a success even if he didn't achieve his goals at work.

The very thought of returning home to a loving partner can wash away much of a man's stress. Then, if he still needs to take some alone time, he won't need to retreat nearly as much.

On the other hand, when a man anticipates arriving home to an unhappy partner, he becomes even more consumed with his work. It is then harder for him to release the pressures of his job.

In my relationship with Bonnie, there are a variety of little things that I can do when I get home to ensure that I get this appreciation. Without much effort at all when I get home, I can find her, give her a hug, ask her about her day, and listen for a few minutes, and I am certain of being appreciated. The more I feel her appreciation and love welcoming me home, the less I need to distract myself from work when I get home. In addition, I tend to acknowledge and recognize my success each day so that I can more easily leave the problems at the office.

Emotional Role Reversal

When a woman is more on her masculine side, and her female side is neglected, an emotional role reversal occurs. She begins to function from the needs of her male side, not her female side. While most modern women can easily recite a litany of valid work- and relationship-related problems and injustices, often the real culprit responsible for their general dissatisfaction is this emotional role reversal.

For women to feel happy in relationships, they need to regain the balance of their male and female sides. Both men and women need to work together to assist the woman in coming back to her female side.

> **A man's new job description requires him to assist a woman in finding her feminine self again after a long day's work.**

The Problems of Emotional Role Reversal

The stress of switching back and forth from the masculine to the feminine side every day has an invisible but devastating effect on lasting romance, passion, and intimacy. Just as a ball rolling downhill gathers speed, so a woman continues to spiral further into frustration if there is no conscious intervention to relieve this stress. Without an understanding of this underlying dynamic, a man's logical attempts to solve partnership problems can be disastrously counterproductive.

When emotional role reversal occurs and a woman is more on her male side, then she automatically feels a greater need to solve problems. It is not enough for her to do what she can do and then relax through talking about everything that is not done. Instead, she feels a strong pull to solve all the unsolved problems before she can relax.

At those times when she feels a need to solve problems, a man can best support her by listening. I remember when I first recognized the symptoms of emotional role reversal in my own marriage but didn't have a clue about correctly supporting my wife.

Bonnie and I had just returned home after playing a really enjoyable tennis game.

"I can't wait to take a nap," I told her.

"That sounds so good," she agreed. "I'd love to take a nap."

As I was walking up the stairs to our bedroom, I noticed that she wasn't behind me and called, "Aren't you coming?"

"I'd love to," she called back, "but I can't. I have to wash the car."

How could she make washing her car more important than taking a nap on a day off? I thought to myself. At this point, I realized we definitely were from different planets.

I did not suspect that she was stuck on her male side and locked into solving her problems. I did not know that nurturing her female side with some conversation would assist her in releasing her burdens and responsibilities. Without an understanding of how I could support her in relaxing, I continued upstairs and instantly dozed.

I woke refreshed and was looking forward to a romantic evening—until I went downstairs and discovered Bonnie in a bad mood.

I casually said, "You should have taken a nap. I feel great." This comment did not go over big.

She responded icily, "I have no time for naps. I still have to do laundry, help with the kids' homework, clean up the house. And I still have to make dinner."

Not realizing that she needed to talk, I continued trying to solve her problems by suggesting we go out for dinner.

"You don't understand," Bonnie insisted, "I have food in the refrigerator that needs to be cooked. And Lauren still hasn't finished her school project."

I said, "This is the weekend. You should be relaxing."

"I can't relax," she said. "You just don't understand!"

At this point I was also in a bad mood. Whatever romance I had inside me quickly dissipated. Bonnie was even more upset because I didn't listen sympathetically, and I was ticked off because she had rejected my solutions.

Now, when Bonnie is feeling overwhelmed, our conversations sound quite different. Instead of feeling rejected or defensive, I know just what to do. She needs to talk to come back to her feminine side, and she needs my help to do it. This is an example of a conversation we might have when Bonnie is overwhelmed and having difficulty switching to her feminine side:

John: "What's wrong?"
Bonnie: "I don't know, there's just too much to do."
John: "Oh."
Bonnie: "I don't have enough time."
John: "Tell me about it."
Bonnie: "I still have to do laundry, and dinner isn't even started."
John: "Hmmm."
Bonnie: "I was supposed to take Pearl to the dentist today and I completely forgot."
John: "What did you do?"
Bonnie: "Oh, I don't even want to think about it."
John: "Hmmm."
Bonnie: "Pearl was so worried, she thought something terrible had happened. (*Pause*) I never forget things like that."

I said nothing, just took a deep breath and shook my head
   back and forth.

Bonnie: "It worked out OK, though. We just rescheduled
   another time."

John: "That's good."

Bonnie: "I don't know what to do about dinner. I haven't
   planned anything."

John: "Hmmm, I don't know either."

Bonnie: "Do you mind eating leftovers tonight?"

John: "Sounds good to me. What do we have?"

Bonnie: "Oh, I don't know. I really don't feel like making
   anything."

John: "Let's just go out to eat, and then we'll have some
   time left for us."

Bonnie: "Great!"

What a difference a few years of practice makes! Without my
knowing how to support Bonnie with the new relationship skill of
nurturing conversation, we would probably just argue, eat leftovers, and go to sleep frustrated and turned off.

Why Women Need More Talk

When, over the course of a relationship, women don't feel free
to talk, they disconnect from the natural happiness that comes
when their female side is nurtured. Even more distressing is the
fact that, as they lose touch with their female side, they may
also lose the awareness of what they need. All they know is
that "something is missing," and generally, the man in their
lives gets blamed.

The more a woman disconnects from her female side, the less
receptive she is to a man's support. Meanwhile, her partner feels
frustrated because he can't fulfill her and feels powerless to change
things.

To cope with the added stress of leaving the home to work, today's woman has a much greater need for partnership support. When she gets home, she needs to talk more. She needs the security of being able to open up and share feelings that may not always make sense or be related to the bottom line. She needs to feel that someone understands what she's going through and cares about her.

This is what happens when a man tries to "solve" a woman's problems:

Anatomy of a Misunderstanding

1. She claims "You are not listening" or "You don't understand."

2. He explains that he was too listening or he couldn't have offered such a great suggestion.

3. She continues to insist that he's not really listening to her and that he doesn't understand her problem.

4. He begins to feel frustrated and tries to prove that he does understand and that his solution is the right one.

5. They begin arguing.

He thinks she is saying that he doesn't understand the problem or that his solution is the wrong one. What she is really saying, though, is that she's not getting the empathy or sympathy she craves. When she says "You don't understand," she really means "You don't understand what I need from you. I just need you to listen and empathize."

Men don't readily know how to respond to work-stressed women because they never saw their fathers do it. In most cases, our mothers spent their days nurturing their feminine natures through communicating with other women. I don't remember ever hearing my mother complain to my dad that "we never talk." By the time Dad came home, she had already talked enough. However, women of our generation don't have this luxury. They are required to be mindful of the time and always to get to the point when talking. They are pushed toward maleness.

One comedian put it this way: God gave women an average of six thousand words a day and men two thousand. Quite commonly, by the end of a workday they have both used two thousand words. When she comes home she still has four thousand left. No wonder she feels neglected. She wants to talk, but he has already spent his allotted two thousand words.

While this is a fun way of understanding the problem, the problem is very real.

> **The lack of communication in relationships
> is the number one reason contemporary women
> are dissatisfied.**

Literally thousands of relationships dramatically improved in an instant as men began to understand the female need to be listened to.

Remember, when men talk about problems, they are generally looking for solutions. Most of the time, however, a man looking to recover from the day doesn't want to talk. The calm he achieves through not talking, women achieve through talking.

In simple terms, a man needs to remember that even when an overwhelmed woman shares a list of problems that demand solutions, the only one that has to be solved immediately is her need to be heard by someone who is not trying to talk her out of her feelings or solve all her problems.

> **Women must remember that when men don't listen
> it is mainly because they don't understand why
> "feeling heard" is so important to women.**

By recognizing that the working world prevents women from nurturing their female sides and finding happiness, men can at last begin to make sense of the feminine need to be heard. Men really do want to make their partners happy, it's just that until now they haven't understood how.

A man can more easily endure the lack of feminine values in the workplace because he has from time immemorial come home from work to a female in order to find balance. But since women rarely work outside the home in a nurturing feminine environment, and they do not have a female to come home to, it is much harder for them to find balance.

Finally, women don't know how to communicate their need for support. Either women expect men to be mind readers and know their needs, or they let their needs build up until they are resentful and then demand more. Neither approach works.

Why Women Don't Like to Ask

Women are wanting more from relationships, even they don't know exactly what they need. In our parents' day, if a man loved a woman he would do what she wanted without being asked.

That is because what she wanted was also what his father taught him to do and her mother told her to expect. He learned from his father how to be a good provider. She didn't have to teach him. Each day he focused on being a better provider. He was not expected to be a domestic helper, and she was not expected to be stressed out and overwhelmed.

When Men Are Self-Motivated

When a man loved a woman according to the old ways, he would provide for her and would willingly give up his life to protect her. That was his most precious gift to her. He did not rely on her to tell him what to do. If he loved her, he motivated himself to provide for her. That self-motivation expressed the extent of his love.

Now women want things our fathers were not required to do. If a woman is to receive a new kind of support, she is required to educate her partner about her needs and to ask in pleasing ways for more.

Having to ask is not easy for women. If she has to ask, then it doesn't feel as if she is being loved. In addition, she really has had very little exposure to a woman asking for what she wants in a way that works. For this reason, I recommend first improving communication, and then beginning to practice the art of asking for more. Once there is good communication and a man begins to understand her feelings more deeply, he will automatically understand her problems better and will slowly but surely do more.

For centuries, the sign that a woman was loved was her not having to ask. Now, when a man appears to a woman as if he is not motivated to support her needs, it weakens her self-esteem and humiliates her. She feels that she is not worthy of his love.

In a similar way, when a man feels that he is unfairly being asked for more, he may not feel that his self-esteem is weakened, but he certainly doesn't feel like giving more. When he returns home from work, he will feel increasingly lifeless and lethargic.

To Ask or Not to Ask

It used to be that the squeaky wheel got oiled. Today, however, the squeaky wheel gets replaced. Asking for more can easily begin to sound like nagging. Men hate to hear it, and women hate to do it. Without understanding how to assist a man in taking the time to listen to her feelings, a woman is left with only two alternatives. She can become a martyr and settle for whatever she gets, or she can try demanding and nagging for more.

Neither alternative will work. To get the love and support she needs, it is crucial for a woman to focus on what is most essential. Ask him to listen, and gradually, over time, as he understands her feelings better, she can begin to ask for more physical support.

> To sustain love and good feelings in a relationship,
> it is vital that a woman learn to express her feelings
> and needs in a way that can work for
> both her man and herself.

I am in no way suggesting that women not express themselves, but I am saying that if they want to be heard and respected, new relationship skills and new job descriptions are definitely required.

What to Expect

When approached in the right way and at the right time, men are happy to do more. With a few months of good communication without demanding anything, and several doses of appreciation, any man will be willing to do more. A man's idea of "more" and a woman's may be dramatically different.

> Men can give more only in small degrees.

It is unrealistic to expect a man suddenly to be motivated to do 50 percent of the housework if he has been used to doing much less. Likewise, if he is the quiet type, it is not probable that he will immediately open up and share his feelings.

It is equally unrealistic for a man to expect his female partner to greet him at home with great appreciation and feel fulfilled when she has also spent all day working. These unrealistic expectations create unnecessary resentment and alienation in both men and women.

Both women and men can get the support they need, but it doesn't happen overnight.

As women begin to accept the fact that they can ask for and get more without having to nag or complain, they give up their resistance to giving a man the daily appreciation he requires. They assume full responsibility for communicating needs, confident that they can get them fulfilled. They don't expect men to know what they need instinctually, but patiently and persistently appreciate what they do give and gradually ask for more.

Adjusting Our Expectations

Just as a woman needs to adjust the expectation that a man will automatically listen to her feelings and will equally share all domestic duties, so also a man must adjust his expectation that a woman will speak in a loving, pleasing manner, make no demands of him, and be fulfilled when he gets home. In essence, women need to release the expectation that men will do everything they want, and men need to release the expectation that women will always be loving and happy.

Through practicing his new relationship skills, instead of feeling annoyed by her feelings of discontent he can begin to see them as opportunities to make her happier. When a woman is not getting the support she wants, she can see it as an opportunity to take the responsibility for getting what she needs. She can view it as an opportunity to practice expressing greater power, but in a feminine way. This is generally something her mother could not tell her.

When a woman is unhappy and talks about problems, a man doesn't have to feel blamed. He can reverse this pattern through understanding her real need to share. When she claims to feel a lack in the relationship, he realizes that it is not because of his deficiency (although it may always sound that way) but because our modern culture doesn't sufficiently support her feminine side. This frees him to truly consider and feel her feelings rather than defend himself. It also greatly clarifies what he is required to do.

When a woman is disappointed by her partner, instead of taking it personally she can reverse the pattern and recognize his loving intent and willingness to support her more, but in small steps. Through adjusting her expectations she can eventually connect with the grace of her feminine spirit, which does not demand perfection but seeks to love and embrace life just the way it is. She realizes that it is not personal but that he was not trained by his father's example in how to fulfill a modern woman's new needs.

3

Men and Their Caves

Without a doubt the most important and useful information for Venusians about Martians is understanding men and their caves. The insight—that a man can love his wife but sometimes not want to spend time with her—is quite surprising for many women and generally very foreign to their nature.

When a woman is in love with her man, she looks forward to spending time together and sharing. Even if she is feeling stressed, she still looks forward to sharing the details of her day with the man she loves. For her, talking and sharing helps to sort things out and release the burdens of the day; it creates intimacy and simply makes her feel better.

For her to connect with her partner and receive his support is one of the major benefits of a relationship. It just feels good when someone who cares also understands what you go through. The more a Venusian loves a man, the more she wants to share with him.

It is very frustrating and disappointing when her beloved Martian comes home and has literally nothing to report. When she asks if something is bothering him, he says, "It's nothing." She doesn't understand that he means, "I'm in my cave for a while, I would rather not talk right now. After a while I'll be out."

....

**A woman mistakenly takes it personally
and feels rejected when a man pulls away
into his cave.**

....

Without understanding that men are from Mars, she can't help but take it personally. She assumes he must not love her if he doesn't want to share with her. Understanding and accepting a man's cave time is essential for every woman who lives with a man, or plans to one day. Although this is much harder than it sounds, these examples may make it easier.

He Still Loves Me

Janet related, "When a girlfriend is mad at me she doesn't want to talk. On Venus, not wanting to talk is the clearest and most definite sign that there is a big problem in the relationship. So when my husband, Carlos, didn't want to talk, I would begin to panic. I would worry about what I had done. Then, after feeling bad for a while, I would get mad that he was rejecting me and I hadn't done anything wrong. Then I would feel hurt.

"Put most simply, when he went to his cave, it was very difficult. When I would want to talk, and he didn't, he would either become bothered by me or just get distracted. When I said he wasn't listening, it just made things worse and we would argue.

"Even though he would tell me nothing was wrong, I didn't believe him. I knew that whenever I didn't want to talk, something was wrong. Reading about the cave has made such a difference. It was a relief to know he still loved me. I couldn't accept that he loved me until I learned that it was not just him, that all Martians regularly go to their caves.

> **I couldn't accept that he loved me until I learned
> that it was not just him, that all Martians regularly
> go to their caves.**

"I was so relieved to discover it didn't mean he loved me less. Before this insight I had felt he didn't love me as much as I loved him. Now I just wait for him to come out of his cave and then I talk. He is usually much more interested. I am so grateful to finally understand my Martian."

It's Not My Fault

Anna shared, "When he was in his cave I always thought I had done something wrong; I thought it was my fault. This made me feel guilty and then I would try to be more pleasing to him. I did everything I could think of. I would try to make the house really clean, I would make his favorite meals, I would not ask for anything more, and then—when he would still go to his cave—I would become very resentful.

> **When he was in his cave I always thought
> I had done something wrong; I thought
> it was my fault.**

"Nothing I did seemed to make a difference. After a while I started to believe that it was my fault that I married the wrong man. Now I am relieved to know I just married a Martian. Instead of doing more for him when he is in his cave, I just ignore him and do things for me. I am still surprised that he is not angry with me. He likes when I give him lots of space. I would prefer to be closer more of the time but this sure beats resenting him.

"It gives me hope to know that as a man matures he gradually needs less time in his cave and as a woman matures she becomes more autonomous and less needy at those times when he is in his cave. I think that the less it bothers me that he is in his cave, the less time he spends in there."

> **The less it bothers me that he is in his cave, the less time he spends in there.**

Venusians Need Caves Too!

Laura had a terrific insight: "Learning to simply accept my partner's need to spend time in his cave has not only created peace in our relationship but it has taught me something very important about myself. Giving him permission to take care of himself at those times gave me permission to take care of myself as well. When I come home from work, instead of jumping into my domestic duties or trying to be the loving wife, I take some time for myself. I figured that if he can do so, then I can too.

> **Giving him permission to take care of himself gave me permission to take care of myself as well.**

"Although my cave looks different from his, it is still time for me and not for anyone else. While he reads a magazine or watches TV, I like to go for a walk or work in my garden. That is my cave. Ironically, by learning to embrace his cave time, I started giving myself what I had always needed but had never given to myself.

"P.S. I am still a Venusian, however; when we are out of the cave, I like to take the time to talk and now he listens."

I Need More Space

Carol had another point of view: "About withdrawing into the cave, it's funny. It's me that does that more than Jack. I need much more privacy than he does. While he was married for all those years, I spent some of my happiest years alone. I seem to need more space. I do think he resents that I go into my cave sometimes, but I've learned to reassure him that I'm going to come back out. It's not really an issue as long as I remember to appreciate the things he does for me. He knows that if I am not attentive to him and his needs because I am in my cave, it is certainly not that I don't appreciate all that he gives me."

I'll Be Back

Janie described how she and her husband changed their behavior: "After reading your books, my husband, Pat, made one small change that has made a big difference in our relationship. He understands that his cave time is hard on me.

"He realized that his pulling away was hard on me. I don't mind working to let him be in his cave, as long as he realizes that it is hard and sometimes it still hurts. When I feel neglected and ignored, he doesn't use the cave as a defense or excuse. Instead he tries to listen and then plans some special time for us.

> When I feel neglected and ignored, he doesn't use the cave as a defense or excuse.

"He doesn't have to give up the cave, but it is nice that he shows that he cares about my feelings. Another way he shows me that he cares is when he says, 'I just need to go for a drive. I'll be back in a little while.' This one comment—'I'll be back'—makes it much easier and I love him for it."

Coming Back from the Cave

Tom revealed his self-doubt: "I have been married thirty-six years and I always thought something was wrong with me. When I heard other men also have a cave, I burst into tears. I had thought I would never be able to really love a woman. I had always felt like such a disappointment to my wife. I would try to be caring and attentive, but inside I just didn't feel it. Nobody ever told me it was okay at those times to just go to my cave.

"Now, when I don't feel warm and loving, I just stop trying and instead do something that I like doing. Many times I just take a nap or go to the movies with a buddy. Then next day, the spell is broken and I am back to loving my wife again. When I pull away, she doesn't feel so disappointed either. That is a relief.

> If I've been in the cave for a few days, when I'm back, I do something special, like bring her flowers or clean up the kitchen.

"I am so grateful that she understands me now even though she doesn't like it very much. After I go to my cave for a while, I always make sure that when I'm back I do something special or show some affection. If I've been in the cave for a few days, I make sure to bring her flowers or clean up the kitchen when I'm back. Doing little things make a big difference and it also lets her know that I am in touch with my loving feelings again."

Having Fun with the Cave

Kyle had a clever solution: "Before taking John's workshop, I would go into my husband's cave and want to decorate it, put up pictures of myself, leave hair clips and nail polish lying around. Though I didn't know it, this was a major violation in Martianville, and Gary kept taking my nesting objects out of his cave. Why didn't he want to be surrounded with the essence of his loving wife? I wanted to know. With an understanding of the cave, I could let go and give him what he needed.

"Gary was excited to know that it was not only okay but mandatory for him to create his own space. One day I came home and heard an intense drilling noise in the back part of the house. It turned out that Gary had put a dead-bolt lock on the room he had designated his cave. Now he could actually lock himself in.

> **Gary was excited to know that it was not only okay but mandatory for him to create his own space.**

"On the outside of his door I hung a big ugly gorilla in the form of a doorbell ornament. Every time you press the button, the gorilla's red eyes light up, his mouth opens, and he makes a roaring sound. Gary threw out my nesting stuff, but he rather liked the gorilla. He and I both understood. We added fun to the cave idea and I learned not to take it personally. Gary needs his cave time. When the door is locked, I don't attempt to enter."

Accepting the Cave

Rose told how she came to understand the cave: "Before I read your book, I was doing everything wrong. When my husband went to his cave I had to follow. I thought I was doing the right thing. I thought it was my job to go in there and get him. If I didn't, then I wasn't a loving wife.

"For over twenty years I have tried everything to get into his cave. I used dynamite to get in. I was a real cave buster!

> I used dynamite to get in.
> I was a real cave buster!

"But when the smoke and dust would clear, I looked around in his cave and he still wasn't there. He was busy digging tunnels to escape me.

"Now I just let him go in there. He comes out all on his own. I've learned the hard way. Anything I do to get him out only makes things worse. When he goes to his cave, I go shopping. We are both so much happier. We are in love again."

Flying Caves

Lynette confessed, "I used to be so hurt when Chris would leave each week for his job. We could spend a wonderful romantic weekend together and then the next day he was off. I was hurt because I thought he loved his work more than me. Even before he left, I started missing him. I was sad but he was happy and excited. I just couldn't understand why he didn't want to spend more time with me.

"Learning about Martians and their need to be on their own, independent and adventurous, helped me not take it so personally when he was excited about leaving. When I learned about the cave, I realized that flying off in airplanes was his way of going to his cave: a flying one. Now, when he is excited about leaving, I realize it is not that he is excited about leaving me; it is that he is excited about going off on an adventure.

"Instead of resenting it when he leaves for a few days, I appreciate that he gets his cave time so that when he is with me, he can be fully here."

Changing Expectations

Krista explained, "Understanding men and their caves changed all my expectations. When he seems distant and aloof I don't panic. It is temporary. I just say 'cancel' to all my automatic responses like, It's my fault, I did something wrong, he doesn't love me, I failed him in some way, he doesn't care for me as much as he used to.

"Now I know he's just doing his Martian thing. It has nothing to do with me. It just means that he has little love to share and that he is taking the time he needs to feel better about himself. He is taking the time he needs for himself so that he will be able to give me the love and attention that I need."

The Man of My Dreams

Lucy recounted, "On May 30, 1991, I met the man of my dreams. His name is Peter Clark. We married a year later, and are now raising his three sons. I am in love with him still. Each morning I am awakened by a man who reaches out for me before he starts his day. And at the end of each hectic day, we are happy just to be in each other's arms again. He understands my Venusian needs and I have learned about his Martian needs. Life is worth living when Venus and Mars are in love.

"But 'bliss' takes work. And, sometimes, skill.

"Peter has many special skills that make me a happy Venusian. For instance, my husband listens to *every word I say*! I know, you couldn't possibly believe me . . . it is so un-Martian! Yet when I ramble on for minutes, half hours, even hours, he listens patiently as I relive and replay every thought and emotion and detail that I went through. He doesn't fidget or get distracted or make me feel that I am imposing on him.

He just listens to the whole thing. He doesn't even offer advice or insight. Peter has been a listening Martian since day one of our relationship. So, of course, *I had to fall in love with him*!

"Learning about his cave has been an enormous help in our relationship. It helps make sense of why sometimes he is so attentive and then at other times he withdraws for days. Before, I used to feel that for some mysterious reason he was rejecting me.

"One evening when he had been withdrawn for several days, I put my arms around his neck and asked, 'Honey, are you in your cave?'

"'Oh, I guess I am,' he replied.

"'It's getting lonely out here,' I told him.

"'Oh, I'm sorry.' And after just a moment's hesitation, he added, 'But I just want you to know that while I was in my cave, your picture was on the wall!'

"But I just want you to know that while I was in my cave, your picture was on the wall!"

"Wow! Spoken loud and clear, right to my Venusian heart! As far as I was concerned, he could go back in his cave for a week, and I'd still know our relationship was important to him."

Commitment in Action

Pam had a story that lasted thirty-five and a half years. "I wanted to share our love story because of its perspective on commitment in action. First, let me introduce myself and my husband. We have been married for thirty-eight and a half years and have five children and five grandchildren. We have had three major career changes—from teaching to owning our own electrical business to pastoring two churches. When we grew to love each other and married, in 1957, my husband had four years of college behind him and two left to go before graduation (he had changed his major). He then went on after his degree to obtain a master's, doctorate, and second bachelor's degree.

"Those early years were marked every two years by the birth of another baby. Still, we remained very much in love, with lots of chemistry and passion. By today's standard we married too young—twenty and twenty-two and a half. But we understood the full meaning of the word 'commitment,' and both agreed it meant a lifetime, no matter what. That commitment has helped us to make peace with our differences.

> **Commitment has helped us to make peace with our differences.**

"We learned after a few years of marriage, to our surprise, that we were totally opposite. He is Mr. Clean and I'm the queen of clutter. He likes to finish everything; I'm open-ended. He has to be alone to charge his battery; I hate to be alone more than an hour or so.

"Although there was conflict, our commitment to make our marriage work helped us to find a solution. The solution always required once again learning to accept and allow the other person to be himself.

"It gives me comfort to understand that when my husband goes into his cave to figure things out, he is being a man, that his retreat has nothing to do with me and that he will be back. We have even joked about him wearing a sign stating, 'In cave/ Out of cave.'

"Once I unknowingly ventured uninvited into his cave and attempted to help him solve a computer problem. Oh, what a mistake! At least I was able to realize why he was so annoyed.

....
**I have gradually learned to accept that he has to be
alone to charge his battery, while I hate to be alone
more than an hour or so.**
....

"Learning to accept and allow Warren to be himself is a
growth process. Differences are not wrong; they keep the passion alive. Warren's need to pull away does not mean he is not
committed to our relationship. Our love for each other has
grown, blossomed, and ripened.

"We have weathered the challenges of education, three
major job changes, five children, male and female differences,
personality and temperament differences, and now, at present,
aging parents . . . only to pay tribute to the word and process
of continual commitment to each other, our love, and making
it work.

"It takes more than *love* to make our marriage work; it
takes commitment, education, skills, insight, and tools. We
supplied the love and commitment, and John Gray supplied
the education, communication skills, insights, and tools."

He Wouldn't Call

Josie learned how to deal with a troubling problem: "Most of
the time, when Harold was out of town working, he wouldn't
call. I couldn't believe that he didn't want to talk with me. I
would feel so hurt that when he came home I wouldn't talk to
him. I just couldn't open up after being ignored this way.

"This was even more confusing for him. He said, 'If you
miss me so much when I am away, then why do you reject me
when I get home. It seems you would be happy to see me because now we can be together.' His 'logical' argument didn't go
over with me.

"After reading John Gray's book, I was able to look at it differently. Before I would take it personally, but now I know it's not that he doesn't want to talk to me but that he is just focused on his work. Even though he doesn't call, he does look forward to coming home and being with me.

"I told him it was okay if he didn't call but that when he did call I would really appreciate it. Now sometimes he calls and sometimes he doesn't. It is no longer a sore spot. When he does call, though, I don't just take it for granted—I make sure to let him know how glad I am."

Controlling Anger

Carolynn described improved communication with her husband. "I am twenty-nine years old and currently a student full-time. My husband, Frank, is thirty-six. Since reading John Gray, our way of communicating has changed. Let's go back to January 1994, when we'd been together for ten years.

"Frank and I truly loved each other all those years, but we had some serious problems. He was a very short-tempered, angry individual, and I was extremely critical and demanding. In January 1994, we experienced the biggest, meanest, and, yes, most violent fight of our relationship. We separated, knowing that we loved each other very much but were just not 'doing it right'—communicating and sharing. Frank joined an 'anger-management group' and I started seeing a therapist. Eight months later, we were happy to say that the dysfunctional part of our relationship had disappeared. Frank was able to use different techniques—for example, time-outs, physical release methods, and so on—to control his anger, and I learned that my judging and critical comments were my own insecurities surfacing.

> We experienced the biggest, meanest, and most
> violent fight of our relationship.

"With the big obstacles out of the way, we thought our relationship would be perfect. Ha-ha! We started having bigger problems ... communication problems. Frank would constantly go into his cave, and I would become resentful and proceed to pull him out. These very serious problems started making us doubt our true love for each other.

"Luckily, my therapist recommended that I read the book. Frank and I made a commitment to read a chapter together every week, but even in the first chapter we were hooked. And since that time, our lives have changed. I let him stay in his cave and know that he is doing what he needs to do so that we can talk later in a more understanding and compassionate manner. We still have arguments, but we learn and grow from them now.

"When I tend to 'go on and on,' Frank understands that I really just need to talk to figure out what's bothering me. He remembers that we are from different planets and doesn't try to 'fix' me. I also have learned that sometimes he will need to go into his cave. I now know that this doesn't mean he doesn't love me or that he won't come back.

"I have heeded Dr. Gray's advice, telling Frank, 'You know, I'm beginning to feel restless and resentful, so I'm going to do something for myself.' And I do; I go shopping or call a friend. This, in turn, takes the pressure off Frank. Just as Dr. Gray mentioned in one of his lectures, the more you practice daily communication techniques, the less often will the man enter his cave, and when he does go in, the less time he will spend there.

> "You know, I'm beginning to feel restless and resentful, so I'm going to do something for myself."

"We still have our high-stress times. However, slowly we become better and better at handling our own emotions. Someone wise once told me, 'Carolynn, it took you and Frank ten years to build this pattern of communication. Give yourself at least half that time to learn, practice, and perfect it.' Thanks to Dr. Gray, we have learned how to do so effectively and sincerely. We truly didn't know how even to attempt good communication before. Both of us learned from our parents that when you are upset with your partner you yell, get angry, hit, and never ever make yourself vulnerable by telling your partner that you're sad or hurt.

"Thank you, Dr. Gray, for writing a book that explains to simply be nice to each other. When you are not exposed to the right way to communicate in a relationship, you simply don't know how. Now we do, and often find ourselves referring to your book."

My Mind Was Glued to the Job

Ross explained that he needed to change. "My wife, Brenda, always used to complain that I wasn't listening to her. She was right. I would try to listen but after a few minutes I went right back to thinking about projects at work. My mind was glued to the job.

"After reading John Gray's book, I realized that I didn't have a cave. When I would come home, my mind was still at the office. I needed some kind of diversion to help me let go of the pressures of work. I needed a cave-time activity.

> I needed some kind of diversion to help me let go of
> the pressures of work.

"Now when I get home I take about twenty minutes to play my keyboard or just listen to some music. It's all I need to relax and forget my deadlines. Then the next thing I do is find Brenda and see if I can help her or start a conversation. Now I can listen to her without being so distracted. She appreciates that I give her my full attention and she doesn't interrupt me when I'm in my cave."

Healthy Intimacy

Candice gained understanding: "I always dreamed that one day I would fall in love with my Prince Charming and we would grow closer as we grew old together. But in reality, I would meet one man after another, but none fit my picture. All the men I met were afraid of intimacy. We would grow close and then they would grow distant. When would I find one who didn't need years of therapy?

"I wanted a man who could open up to me and share his heart and soul. I wanted to be a team. We would always come together to share our feelings, problems, and needs. Someone who depended on me and I on him. It seemed in every relationship after a few months the man would back off in some way. When I tried to get him to talk, there was always 'nothing' to talk about or he would feel smothered.

"I was so surprised to find that these men were not afraid of intimacy, nor did they need years of therapy—they were from Mars. What a difference it has made for me! Now, when my boyfriend pulls back, I don't panic and definitely I don't ask him a bunch of questions or try to get him to talk.

> **Men were not afraid of intimacy, nor did they need years of therapy—they were from Mars.**

"I am now in a beautiful relationship. Much of the time it is just what I want and at other times I just let go and trust that he will come out of his cave on his own. Much to my surprise, he does. I had always thought that the men in my life had run away from me. Through understanding men and their caves, I learned how I had been pushing them away. I am grateful to have a new model of healthy intimacy, which is achieved through a balance of alone time and together time, a loving blend of being independent and dependent—interdependence."

How Long in the Cave Is Too Long?

Sally needed signals. "I used to wonder how long in the cave is too long. Gradually I realized that there is no right amount of time. Sometimes it is weeks and other times it is just hours. What was most frustrating for me was to not know when he was out. I didn't want to be ignoring him and giving him space if he was out of the cave.

> **What was most frustrating for me was to not know when he was out of the cave.**

"I liked your idea of having clear signals. Now, when he is out of his cave, he lets me know. He starts touching me and being affectionate. He also knows the longer he has been in the cave, the more romance I need to fully open up again to him. It is hard not to take it personally when suddenly I am being ignored. Learning to give to myself at those times not only frees him from feeling pressured, but has helped me be less needy. I clearly see that the more I can let go of needing intimacy when he pulls away, the easier it is for him to come out."

Repeating My Parents' Marriage

Mary realized she had an option. "When I married Stephen, I didn't want my marriage to look like my parents' marriage. But after a few years I found myself doing the same things my mother did.

"I am sure that she did what she did because she didn't know another way. When my dad went to his cave, Mom would nag him, complain to him, ask lots of questions, and then criticize him for pulling away. She blamed him for her unhappiness and eventually withdrew herself and stopped talking.

> **When my dad went to his cave,**
> **Mom would nag him, complain to him,**
> **ask lots of questions, and then criticize**
> **him for pulling away.**

"I promised myself that we would talk and work things out. But I still didn't understand the cave. So, when Stephen withdrew, I would try to get him to talk. Eventually I found myself nagging, complaining, and asking him lots of questions—just like Mom. I felt he was not cooperating and eventually started to blame him. I realized I had married my father and I had become my mother.

"I discovered that he was *not* my father, but they were both related—they were from Mars. Reading John Gray has given me a choice. Before I didn't really have an option, I just did what she did."

4

Understanding Martian/Venusian

When the Martians and Venusians first got together, they encountered many of the problems with relationships we have today. Because they recognized that they were different, they were able to solve these problems. One of the secrets of their success was good communication.

Ironically, they communicated well because they spoke different languages. When they had problems, they would just go to a translator for assistance. Everyone knew that people from Mars and people from Venus spoke different languages, so when there was a conflict they didn't start judging or fighting but instead pulled out their phrase dictionaries to understand each other more fully. If that didn't work they went to a translator for help.

The Martian and Venusian languages had the same words, but the way they were used gave different meanings.

You see the Martian and Venusian languages had the same words, but the way they were used gave different meanings. Their expressions were similar, but they had different connotations or emotional emphasis. Misinterpreting each other was very easy. So when communication problems emerged, they assumed it was just one of those expected misunderstandings and that with a little assistance they would surely understand each other. They experienced a trust and acceptance that we rarely experience today.

Expressing Feelings Versus Expressing Information

Even today we still need translators. Men and women seldom mean the same things even when they use the same words. For example, when a woman says "I feel like you *never* listen," she does not expect the word *never* to be taken literally. Using the word *never* is just a way of expressing the frustration she is feeling at the moment. It is not to be taken as if it were factual information.

> **To fully express their feelings, women
> assume poetic license to use various superlatives,
> metaphors, and generalizations.**

To fully express their feelings, women assume poetic license and use various superlatives, metaphors, and generalizations. Men mistakenly take these expressions literally. Because they misunderstand the intended meaning, they commonly react in an unsupportive manner. In the following chart ten complaints easily misinterpreted are listed, as well as how a man might respond unsupportively.

Ten Common Complaints that Are Easily Misinterpreted

Women say things like this	*Men respond like this*
"We never go out."	"That's not true. We went out last week."
"Everyone ignores me."	"I'm sure some people notice you."
"I am so tired, I can't do anything."	"That's ridiculous. You are not helpless."
"I want to forget everything."	"If you don't like your job, then quit."

"The house is always a mess."	"It's not always a mess."
"No one listens to me anymore."	"But I am listening to you right now."
"Nothing is working."	"Are you saying it is my fault?"
"You don't love me anymore."	"Of course I do. That's why I'm here."
"We are always in a hurry."	"We are not. Friday we were relaxed."
"I want more romance."	"Are you saying I am not romantic?"

You can see how a "literal" translation of a woman's words could easily mislead a man who is used to using speech as a means of conveying only facts and information. We can also see how a man's responses might lead to an argument. Unclear and unloving communication is the biggest problem in relationships. The number one complaint women have in relationships is: "I don't feel heard." Even this complaint is misunderstood and misinterpreted!

The number one complaint women have in relationships is: "I don't feel heard." Even this complaint is misunderstood by men!

A man's literal translation of "I don't feel heard" leads him to invalidate and argue with her feelings. He thinks he *has* heard her if he can repeat what she has said. A translation of a woman saying "I don't feel heard" so that a man could correctly interpret it is: "I feel as though you don't fully understand what I really mean to say or care about how I feel. Would you show me that you are interested in what I have to say?"

If a man really understood her complaint then he would argue less and be able to respond more positively. When men and women are on the verge of arguing, they are generally misunderstanding each other. At such times, it is important to rethink or translate what they have heard.

Because many men don't understand that women express feelings differently, they inappropriately judge or invalidate their partner's feelings. This leads to arguments. The ancient Martians learned to avoid many arguments through correct understanding. Whenever listening stirred up some resistance, they consulted their *Venusian/Martian Phrase Dictionary* for a correct interpretation.

When Venusians Talk

The following section contains various excerpts from the lost *Venusian/Martian Phrase Dictionary*. Each of the ten complaints listed above is translated so that a man can understand their real and intended meaning. Each translation also contains a hint of how she wants him to respond.

You see, when a Venusian is upset she not only uses generalities, and so forth, but also is asking for a particular kind of support. She doesn't directly ask for that support because on Venus everyone knew that dramatic language implied a particular request.

In each of the translations this hidden request for support is revealed. If a man listening to a woman can recognize the implied request and respond accordingly, she will feel truly heard and loved.

The Venusian/Martian Phrase Dictionary

"**We never go out**" translated into Martian means "I feel like going out and doing something together. We always have such a fun time, and I love being with you. What do you think? Would you take me out to dinner? It has been a few days since we went out."

Without this translation, when a woman says "We never go out" a man may hear "You are not doing your job. What a disappointment you have turned out to be. We never do anything together anymore because you are lazy, unromantic, and just boring."

"Everyone ignores me" translated into Martian means "Today, I am feeling ignored and unacknowledged. I feel as though nobody sees me. Of course I'm sure some people see me, but they don't seem to care about me. I suppose I am also disappointed that you have been so busy lately. I really do appreciate how hard you are working and sometimes I start to feel like I am not important to you. I am afraid your work is more important than me. Would you give me a hug and tell me how special I am to you?"

Without this translation, when a woman says "Everyone ignores me" a man may hear "I am so unhappy. I just can't get the attention I need. Everything is completely hopeless. Even you don't notice me, and you are the person who is supposed to love me. You should be ashamed. You are so unloving. I would never ignore you this way."

"I am so tired, I can't do anything" translated into Martian means "I have been doing so much today. I really need a rest before I can do anything more. I am so lucky to have your support. Would you give me a hug and reassure me that I am doing a good job and that I deserve a rest?"

Without this translation, when a woman says "I am so tired, I can't do anything" a man may hear "I do everything and you do nothing. You should do more. I can't do it all. I feel so hopeless. I want a 'real man' to live with. Picking you was a big mistake."

"I want to forget everything" translated into Martian means "I want you to know that I love my work and my life but today I am so overwhelmed. I would love to do something really nurturing for myself before I have to be responsible again. Would you ask me 'What's the matter?' and then listen with empathy without offering any solutions? I just want to feel you understanding the pressures I feel. It would make me feel so much better. It helps me to relax. Tomorrow I will get back to being responsible and handling things."

Without this translation, when a woman says "I want to forget everything" a man may hear "I have to do so much that I don't want to do. I am so unhappy with you and our relationship. I want a better partner who can make my life more fulfilling. You are doing a terrible job."

"This house is always a mess" translated into Martian means "Today I feel like relaxing, but the house is so messy. I am frustrated and I need a rest. I hope you don't expect me to clean it all up. Would you agree with me that it is a mess and then offer to help clean up part of it?"

Without this translation, when a woman says "This house is always a mess" a man may hear "This house is a mess because of you. I do everything possible to clean it up, and before I have finished, you have messed it up again. You are a lazy slob and I don't want to live with you unless you change. Clean up or clear out!"

"No one listens to me anymore" translated into Martian means "I am afraid I am boring to you. I am afraid you are no longer interested in me. I seem to be very sensitive today. Would you give me some special attention? I would love it. I've had a hard day and feel as though no one wants to hear what I have to say.

"Would you listen to me and continue to ask me supportive questions such as: 'What happened today? What else happened? How did you feel? What did you want? How else do you feel?' Also support me by saying caring, acknowledging, and reassuring statements such as: 'Tell me more' or 'That's right' or 'I know what you mean' or 'I understand.' Or just listen, and occasionally when I pause make one of these reassuring sounds: 'oh,' 'humph,' 'uh-huh,' and 'hmmm.'" *(Note: Martians had never heard of these sounds before arriving on Venus.)*

Without this translation, when a woman says "No one listens to me anymore" he may hear "I give you my attention but you don't listen to me. You used to. You have become a very boring person to be with. I want someone exciting and interesting and you are definitely not that person. You have disappointed me. You are selfish, uncaring, and bad."

"Nothing is working" translated into Martian means "Today I am so overwhelmed *and* I am so grateful that I can share my feelings with you. It helps me so much to feel better. Today it seems like nothing I do works. I know that this is not true, but I sure feel that way when I get so overwhelmed by all the things I still have to do. Would you give me a hug and tell me that I am doing a great job. It would sure feel good."

Without this translation, when a woman says "Nothing is working" a man may hear "You never do anything right. I can't trust you. If I hadn't listened to you I wouldn't be in this mess. Another man would have fixed things, but you made them worse."

"You don't love me anymore" translated into Martian means "Today I am feeling as though you don't love me. I am afraid I have pushed you away. I know you really do love me, you do so much for me. Today I am just feeling a little insecure. Would you reassure me of your love and tell me those three magic words, I love you. When you do that it feels so good."

Without this translation, when a woman says "You don't love me anymore" a man may hear "I have given you the best years of my life, and you have given me nothing. You used me. You are selfish and cold. You do what you want to do, for you and only you. You do not care about anybody. I was a fool for loving you. Now I have nothing."

"We are always in a hurry" translated into Martian means "I feel so rushed today. I don't like rushing. I wish our life was not so hurried. I know it is nobody's fault and I certainly don't blame you. I know you are doing your best to get us there on time and I really appreciate how much you care.

"Would you empathize with me and say something like, 'It *is* hard always rushing around. I don't always like rushing either.'"

Without this translation, when a woman says "We are always in a hurry" a man may hear "You are so irresponsible. You wait until the last minute to do everything. I can never be happy when I am with you. We are always rushing to avoid being late. You ruin things every time I am with you. I am so much happier when I am not around you."

"I want more romance" translated into Martian means "Sweetheart, you have been working so hard lately. Let's take some time out for ourselves. I love it when we can relax and be alone without the kids around and no work pressures. You are so romantic. Would you surprise me with flowers sometime

soon and take me out on a date? I love being ro-
manced."

Without this translation, when a woman says "I want more
romance" a man may hear "You don't satisfy me anymore. I am
not turned on to you. Your romantic skills are definitely inade-
quate. You have never really fulfilled me. I wish you were more
like other men I have been with."

After using this dictionary for a few years, a man doesn't need
to pick it up each time he feels blamed or criticized. He begins to
understand the way women think and feel. He learns that these
kinds of dramatic phrases are not to be taken literally. They are
just the way women express feeling more fully. That's the way it
was done on Venus and people from Mars need to remember that!

When Martians Don't Talk

One of the big challenges for men is correctly to interpret and support a woman when she is talking about her feelings. The biggest
challenge for women is correctly to interpret and support a man
when he isn't talking. Silence is most easily misinterpreted by
women.

> **The biggest challenge for women
> is correctly to interpret and support a man
> when he *isn't* talking.**

Quite often a man will suddenly stop communicating and become silent. This was unheard of on Venus. At first a woman
thinks the man is deaf. She thinks that maybe he doesn't hear
what's being said and that is why he is not responding.

You see men and women think and process information
very differently. Women think out loud, sharing their process of
inner discovery with an interested listener. Even today, a
woman often discovers what she wants to say through the

process of just talking. This process of just letting thoughts flow freely and expressing them out loud helps her to tap into her intuition. This process is perfectly normal and especially necessary sometimes.

But men process information very differently. Before they talk or respond, they first silently "mull over" or think about what they have heard or experienced. Internally and silently they figure out the most correct or useful response. They first formulate it inside and then express it. This process could take from minutes to hours. And to make matters even more confusing for women, if he does not have enough information to process an answer, a man may not respond at all.

Women need to understand that when he is silent, he is saying "I don't know what to say yet, but I am thinking about it." Instead what they hear is "I am not responding to you because I don't care about you and I am going to ignore you. What you have said to me is not important and therefore I am not responding."

How She Reacts to His Silence

Women misinterpret a man's silence. Depending on how she is feeling that day she may begin to imagine the very worst—"He hates me, he doesn't love me, he is leaving me forever." This may then trigger her deepest fear, which is "I am afraid that if he rejects me then I will never be loved. I don't deserve to be loved."

When a man is silent it is easy for a woman to imagine the worst because the only times a woman would be silent are when what she had to say would be hurtful or when she didn't want to talk to a person because she didn't trust him anymore and wanted to have nothing to do with him. No wonder women become insecure when a man suddenly becomes quiet!

**When a man is silent it is easy
for a woman to imagine the worst.**

When a woman listens to another woman, she will continue to reassure the speaker that she is listening and that she cares. Instinctively when the speaker pauses the female listener will reassure the speaker by making reassuring responses like "oh, uh-huh, hmmm, ah, ah-ha, or humph."

Without these reassuring responses, a man's silence can be very threatening. In the last chapter, we explored the concept of a man's cave. And through understanding, women can learn to interpret a man's silence correctly, and to respond to it.

Understanding the Cave

Women have a lot to learn about men before their relationships can be really fulfilling. They need to learn that when a man is upset or stressed he will automatically stop talking and go to his "cave" to work things out. They need to learn that no one is allowed in that cave, not even the man's best friends. This was the way it was on Mars. Women should not become scared that they have done something terribly wrong. They need gradually to learn that if you just let men go into their caves, after a while they will come out and everything will be fine.

This lesson is difficult for women because on Venus one of the golden rules was never to abandon a friend when she was upset. It just doesn't seem loving to abandon her favorite Martian when he is upset. Because she cares for him, a woman wants to come into his cave and offer him help.

In addition, she often mistakenly assumes that if she could ask him lots of questions about how he is feeling and be a good listener, then he would feel better. This only upsets Martians more. She instinctively wants to support him in the way that she would want to be supported. Her intentions are good, but the outcome is counterproductive.

Both men and women need to stop offering the method of caring they would prefer and start to learn the different ways their partners think, feel, and react.

Remember Why Men Go into Their Caves

Men go into their caves or become quiet for a variety of reasons.

1. He needs to think about a problem and find a practical solution to the problem.

2. He doesn't have an answer to a question or a problem. Men were never taught to say, "Gee, I don't have an answer. I need to go into my cave and find one." Other men assume he is doing just that when he becomes quiet.

3. He has become upset or stressed. At such times he needs to be alone to cool off and find his control again. He doesn't want to do or say anything he might regret.

4. He needs to find himself. This fourth reason becomes very important when men are in love. At times they begin to lose and forget themselves. They can feel that too much intimacy robs them of their power. They need to regulate how close they get. Whenever they get too close so as to lose themselves, alarm bells go off and they are on their way into the cave. As a result they are rejuvenated and find their loving and powerful self again.

Why Women Talk

Women talk for a variety of reasons. Sometimes women talk for the same reasons that men stop talking. These are four common reasons that women talk:

1. To convey or gather information. (This is generally the only reason a man talks.)

2. To explore and discover what it is she wants to say. (He stops talking to figure out inside what he wants to say. She talks to think out loud.)

3. To feel better and more centered when she is upset. (He stops talking when he is upset. In his cave he has a chance to cool off.)

4. To create intimacy. Through sharing her inner feelings she is able to know her loving self. (A Martian stops talking to find himself again. Too much intimacy, he fears, will rob him of himself.)

Without this vital understanding of our differences and needs it is easy to see why couples struggle so much in relationships.

Getting Burned by the Dragon

As we discussed earlier, it is important for women to understand not to try and get a man to talk before he is ready. While discussing this topic in one of my seminars, a Native American shared that in her tribe mothers would instruct young women getting married to remember that when a man was upset or stressed he would withdraw into his cave. She was not to take it personally because it would happen from time to time. It did not mean that he did not love her. They assured her that he would come back. But most important they warned the young woman never to follow him into his cave. If she did then she would get burned by the dragon who protected the cave.

> **Remember, never go into a man's cave or you will be burned by the dragon!**

Much unnecessary conflict has resulted from a woman following a man into his cave. Women just haven't understood that men really do need to be alone or silent when they are upset. When a man withdraws into his cave a woman just doesn't understand what is happening. She naturally tries to get him to talk. If there is a problem she hopes to nurture him by drawing him out and getting him to talk about it.

She asks "Is there something wrong?" He says "No." But she can feel he is upset. She wonders why he is withholding his feelings. Instead of letting him work it out inside his cave she unknowingly interrupts his internal process. She asks again, "I know something is bothering you, what is it?"

He says "It's nothing."

She asks "It's not nothing. Something's bothering you. What are you feeling?"

He says "Look, I'm fine. Now leave me alone!"

She says "How can you treat me like this? You never talk to me anymore. How am I supposed to know what you are feeling? You don't love me. I feel so rejected by you."

At this point he loses control and begins saying things that he will regret later. His dragon comes out and burns her.

When Martians Do Talk

Women get burned not only when they unknowingly invade a man's introspective time but also when they misinterpret his expressions, which are generally warnings that he is either in his cave or on his way to the cave. When asked "What's the matter?" a Martian will say something brief like "It's nothing" or "I am OK."

These brief signals are generally the only way a Venusian knows to give him space to work out his feelings alone. Instead of saying "I am upset and I need some time to be alone," men just become quiet.

In the following chart six commonly expressed abbreviated warning signals are listed as well as how a woman might unknowingly respond in an intrusive and unsupportive manner:

Six Common Abbreviated Warning Signals

When a woman asks , "What's the matter?"

A man says	*A woman may respond*
"I'm OK" or "It's OK."	"I know something's wrong. What is it?"
"I'm fine" or "It's fine."	"But you seem upset. Let's talk."
"It's nothing."	"I want to help. I know something is bothering you. What is it?"
"It's all right" or "I'm all right."	"Are you sure? I am happy to help you."
"It's no big deal."	"But something is upsetting you. I think we should talk."
"It's no problem."	"But it is a problem. I could help."

When a man makes one of the above abbreviated comments he generally wants silent acceptance or space. At times like this, to avoid misinterpretation and unnecessary panic, the Venusians consulted their *Martian/Venusian Phrase Dictionary*. Without this assistance, women misinterpret these abbreviated expressions.

Women need to know that when a man says "I am OK" it is an abbreviated version of what he really means, which is "I am OK because I can deal with this alone. I do not need any help. Please support me by not worrying about me. Trust that I can deal with it all by myself."

Without this translation, when he is upset and says "I am OK" it sounds to her as if he is denying his feelings or problems. She then attempts to help him by asking questions or talking about what she thinks the problem is. She does not know that he is speaking an abbreviated language. The following are excerpts from their phrase dictionary.

The Martian/Venusian Phrase Dictionary

"**I'm OK**" translated into Venusian means "I am OK, I can deal with my upset. I don't need any help, thank you."

Without this translation, when he says "I am OK" she may hear "I am not upset because I do not care" or she may hear "I am not willing to share with you my upset feelings. I do not trust you to be there for me."

"**I'm fine**" translated into Venusian means "I am fine because I am successfully dealing with my upset or problem. I don't need any help. If I do I will ask."

Without this translation, when he says "I am fine" she may hear "I don't care about what has happened. This problem is not important to me. Even if it upsets you, I don't care."

"**It's nothing**" translated into Venusian means "Nothing is bothering me that I cannot handle alone. Please don't ask any more questions about it."

Without this translation, when he says "Nothing is bothering me" she may hear "I don't know what is bothering me. I need you to ask me questions to assist me in discovering what is happening." At this point she proceeds to anger him by asking questions when he really wants to be left alone.

"**It's all right**" translated into Venusian means "This is a problem but you are not to blame. I can resolve this within myself if you don't interrupt my process by asking more questions or offering suggestions. Just act like it didn't happen and I can process it within myself more effectively."

Without this translation, when he says "It's all right" she may hear "This is the way it is supposed to be. Nothing needs to be changed. You can abuse me and I can abuse you" or she hears "It's all right this time, but remember it is your fault. You can do this once but don't do it again, or else."

> **"It's no big deal"** translated into Venusian means "It is no big deal because I can make things work again. Please don't dwell on this problem or talk more about it. That makes me more upset. I accept responsibility for solving this problem. It makes me happy to solve it."

Without this translation, when he says "It's no big deal" she may hear "You are making a big deal out of nothing. What concerns you is not important. Don't overreact."

> **"It's no problem"** translated into Venusian means "I have no problem doing this or solving this problem. It is my pleasure to offer this gift to you."

Without this translation, when he says "It's no problem" she may hear "This is not a problem. Why are you making it a problem or asking for help?" She then mistakenly explains to him why it is a problem.

Using this *Martian/Venusian Phrase Dictionary* can assist women in understanding what men really mean when they abbreviate what they are saying. Sometimes what he is really saying is the opposite of what she hears.

What to Do When He Goes into His Cave

In my seminars when I explain about caves and dragons, women want to know how they can shorten the time men spend in their caves. At this point I ask the men to answer, and they generally say that the more women try to get them to talk or come out, the longer it takes.

Another common comment by men is "It is hard to come out of the cave when I feel my mate disapproves of the time I spend in the cave." To make a man feel wrong for going into his cave has the effect of pushing him back into the cave even when he wants to come out.

When a man goes into his cave he is generally wounded or stressed and is trying to solve his problem alone. To give him the support that a woman would want is counterproductive. There are basically six ways to support him when he goes into his cave. (Giving him this support will also shorten the time he needs to spend alone.)

How to Support a Man in His Cave

1. Don't disapprove of his need for withdrawing.
2. Don't try to help him solve his problem by offering solutions.
3. Don't try to nurture him by asking questions about his feelings.
4. Don't sit next to the door of the cave and wait for him to come out.
5. Don't worry about him or feel sorry for him.
6. Do something that makes you happy.

If you need to "talk," write him a letter to be read later when he is out, and if you need to be nurtured, talk to a friend. Don't make him the sole source of your fulfillment.

A man wants his favorite Venusian to trust that *he* can handle what is bothering him. To be trusted that he can handle his problems is very important to his honor, pride, and self-esteem.

Not worrying about him is difficult for her. Worrying for others is one way women express their love and caring. It is a way of showing love. For a woman, being happy when the person you love is upset just doesn't seem right. He certainly doesn't want her to be happy *because* he is upset, but he does want her to be happy. He wants her to be happy so that he has one less problem to worry about. In addition he wants her to be happy because it helps him to feel loved by her. When a woman is happy and free from worry, it is easier for him to come out.

Ironically men show their love by not worrying. A man questions, "How can you worry about someone whom you admire and trust?" Men commonly support one another by saying phrases such as "Don't worry, you can handle it" or "That's their problem, not yours" or "I'm sure it will work out." Men support one another by not worrying or minimizing their troubles.

It took me years to understand that my wife actually wanted me to worry for her when she was upset. Without this awareness of our different needs, I would minimize the importance of her concerns. This only made her more upset.

When a man goes into his cave he is generally trying to solve a problem. If his mate is happy or *not* needy at this time, then he has one less problem to solve before coming out. Knowing that she is happy with him also gives him more strength to deal with his problem while in the cave.

Anything that distracts her or helps her to feel good will be helpful to him. These are some examples:

Read a book	Call a girlfriend for a
Listen to music	good chat
Work in the garden	Write in a journal
Exercise	Go shopping
Get a massage	Pray or meditate
Listen to self-	Go for a walk
improvement tapes	Take a bubble bath
Treat yourself to	See a therapist
something delicious	Watch TV or a video

The Martians also recommended that the Venusians do something enjoyable. It was hard to conceive of being happy when a friend was hurting, but the Venusians did find a way. Every time their favorite Martian went into his cave, they would go shopping or out on some other pleasing excursion. Venusians love to shop. My wife, Bonnie, sometimes uses this technique. When she sees I am in my cave, she goes shopping. I never feel like I have to apologize for my Martian side. When she can take care of herself I feel OK taking care of myself and going into my cave. She trusts that I will come back and be more loving.

She knows that when I go into my cave it is not the right time to talk. When I begin showing signs of interest in her, she recognizes that I am coming out of the cave, and it is then a time to talk. Sometimes she will casually say, "When you feel like talking, I would like to spend some time together. Would you let me know when?" In this way she can test the waters without being pushy or demanding.

How to Communicate Support to a Martian

Even when they are out of the cave men want to be trusted. They don't like unsolicited advice or empathy. They need to prove themselves. Being able to accomplish things without the help of others is a feather in their cap. (While for a woman, when someone assists her, having a supportive relationship is a feather in her cap.) A man feels supported when a woman communicates in a way that says "I trust you to handle things unless you directly ask for help."

Learning to support men in this way can be very difficult in the beginning. Many women feel that the only way they can get what they need in a relationship is to criticize a man when he makes mistakes and to offer unsolicited advice. Without a role model of a mother who knew how to receive support from a man, it does not occur to women that they can encourage a man to give more by directly asking for support—without being critical or offering advice. In addition, if he behaves in a manner that she does not like she can simply and directly tell him that she doesn't like his behavior, without casting judgment that he is wrong or bad.

How to Approach a Man with Criticism or Advice

Without an understanding of how they are turning men off with unsolicited advice and criticism, many women feel powerless to get what they need and want from a man. Nancy was frustrated in her relationships. She said, "I still don't know how to approach a man with criticism and advice. What if his table manners are atrocious or he dresses really, really badly? What if he's a nice guy but you see he's got a pattern of behaving with people in a way that makes him look like a jerk and that's causing him trouble in relationships with others? What should I do? No matter how I tell him, he gets angry or defensive or just ignores me."

The answer is that she should definitely not offer criticism or advice unless he asks. Instead, she should try giving him loving acceptance. This is what he needs, not lectures. As he begins to feel her acceptance, he will begin to ask what she thinks. If, however, he detects her demanding that he change, he will not ask for advice or suggestions. Especially in an intimate relationship, men need to feel very secure before they open up and ask for support.

In addition to patiently trusting her partner to grow and change, if a woman is not getting what she needs and wants, she can and should share her feelings and make requests (but again without giving advice or criticism). This is an art that requires caring and creativity. These are four possible approaches:

1. A woman can tell a man that she doesn't like the way he dresses without giving him a lecture on how to dress. She could say casually as he is getting dressed "I don't like that shirt on you. Would you wear another one tonight?" If he is annoyed by that comment, then she should respect his sensitivities and apologize. She could say "I'm sorry— I didn't mean to tell you how to dress."

2. If he is that sensitive—and some men are—then she could try talking about it at another time. She could say "Remember that blue shirt you wore with the green

_ks? I didn't like that combination. Would you try wearing it with your gray slacks?"

3. She could directly ask "Would you let me take you shopping one day? I would love to pick out an outfit for you." If he says no, then she can be sure that he doesn't want any more mothering. If he says yes, be sure not to offer too much advice. Remember his sensitivities.

4. She could say "There is something I want to talk about but I don't know how to say it. [*Pause.*] I don't want to offend you, but I also really want to say it. Would you listen and then suggest to me a better way I could say it?" This helps him to prepare himself for the shock and then he happily discovers that it is not such a big deal.

Let's explore another example. If she doesn't like his table manners and they are alone, she could say (without a disapproving look) "Would you use your silverware?" or "Would you drink from your glass?" If, however, you are in front of others, it is wise to say nothing and not even notice. Another day you could say "Would you use your silverware when we eat in front of the kids?" or "When you eat with your fingers, I hate it. I get so picky about these little things. When you eat with me, would you use your silverware?"

If he behaves in a way that embarrasses you, wait for a time when no one else is around and then share your feelings. Don't tell him how he "should behave" or that he is wrong; instead share honest feelings in a loving and brief way. You could say "The other night at the party, I didn't like it when you were so loud. When I'm around, would you try to keep it down?" If he gets upset and doesn't like this comment, then simply apologize for being critical.

When a Man Doesn't Need Help

A man may start to feel smothered when a woman tries to comfort him or help him solve a problem. He feels as though she doesn't trust him to handle his problems. He may feel controlled, as if she is treating him like a child, or he may feel she wants to change him.

This doesn't mean that a man does not need comforting love. Women need to understand that they are nurturing him when they abstain from offering unsolicited advice to solve his problems. He needs her loving support but in a different way than she thinks. To withhold correcting a man or trying to improve him are ways to nurture him. Giving advice can be nurturing only if he directly asks for it.

A man looks for advice or help only after he has done what he can do alone. If he receives too much assistance or receives it too soon, he will lose his sense of power and strength. He becomes either lazy or insecure. Instinctively men support one another by not offering advice or help unless specifically approached and asked.

In coping with problems, a man knows he has to first go a certain distance by himself, and then if he needs help he can ask for it without losing his strength, power, and dignity. To offer help to a man at the wrong time could easily be taken as an insult.

When a man is carving the turkey for Thanksgiving and his partner keeps offering advice on how and what to cut, he feels mistrusted. He resists her and is determined to do it his way on his own. On the other hand, if a man offers her assistance in cutting the turkey she feels loved and cared for.

While men want to be trusted, women want caring. When a man says to a woman "What's the matter, honey?" with a concerned look on his face, she feels comforted by his caring. When a woman in a similar caring and concerned way says to a man "What's the matter, honey?" he may feel insulted or repulsed. He feels as though she doesn't trust him to handle things.

It is very difficult for a man to differentiate between empathy and sympathy. He hates to be pitied. A woman may say "I am so sorry I hurt you." He will say "It was no big deal" and push away her support. She on the other hand loves to hear him say "I'm sorry I hurt you." She then feels he really cares. Men need to find ways to show they care while women need to find ways to show they trust.

> It is very difficult for a man to differentiate
> between empathy and sympathy.
> He hates to be pitied.

Too Much Caring Is Smothering

When I first married Bonnie, the night before I would leave town to teach a weekend seminar, she would ask me what time I was getting up. Then she would ask what time my plane left. Then she would do some mental figuring and warn me that I hadn't left enough time to catch my plane. Each time she thought she was supporting me, but I didn't feel it. I felt offended. I had been traveling around the world for fourteen years teaching courses, and I had never missed a plane.

Then in the morning, before I left, she asked me a string of questions such as, "Do you have your ticket? Do you have your wallet? Do you have enough money? Did you pack socks? Do you know where you are staying?" She thought she was loving me, but I felt mistrusted and was annoyed. Eventually I let her know that I appreciated her loving intention but that I didn't like being mothered in this way.

I shared with her that if she wanted to mother me, then the way I wanted to be mothered was to be unconditionally loved and trusted. I said, "If I miss a plane, don't tell me 'I told you so.' Trust that I will learn my lesson and adjust accordingly. If I forget my toothbrush or shaving kit, let me deal with it. Don't tell me about it when I call." With an awareness of what I wanted, instead of what she would have wanted, it was easier for her to succeed in supporting me.

A Success Story

Once, on a trip to Sweden to teach my relationship seminar, I called back to California from New York, informing Bonnie that I had left my passport at home. She reacted in such a beautiful and loving way. She didn't lecture me on being more responsible.

Instead she laughed and said, "Oh my goodness, John, you have such adventures. What are you going to do?"

I asked her to fax my passport to the Swedish consulate, and the problem was solved. She was so cooperative. Never once did she succumb to lecturing me on being more prepared. She was even proud of me for finding a solution to my problem.

Making Little Changes

One day I noticed that when my children asked me to do things I would always say "no problem." It was my way of saying I would be happy to do that. My stepdaughter Julie asked me one day, "Why do you always say 'no problem'?" I didn't actually know right away. After a while I realized that it was another of those deeply ingrained Martian habits. With this new awareness I started saying "I would be happy to do that." This phrase expressed my implied message and certainly felt more loving to my Venusian daughter.

This example symbolizes a very important secret for enriching relationships. Little changes can be made without sacrificing who we are. This was the secret of success for the Martians and Venusians. They were both careful not to sacrifice their true natures, but they were also willing to make small changes in the way they interacted. They learned how relationships could work better by creating or changing a few simple phrases.

The important point here is that to enrich our relationships we need to make little changes. Big changes generally require some suppression of who we truly are. This is not good.

Giving some reassurance when he goes into his cave is a small change that a man can make without changing his nature. To make this change he must realize that women really do need some reassurance, especially if they are to worry less. If a man doesn't understand the differences between men and women, then he cannot comprehend why his sudden silence is such a cause for worry. By giving some reassurance he can remedy the situation.

On the other hand if he does not know how he is different, then when she is upset by his tendency to go into his cave, he may give up going into his cave in an attempt to fulfill her. This is a big mistake. If he gives up the cave (and denies his true nature) he becomes irritable, overly sensitive, defensive, weak, passive, or mean. And to make matters worse, he doesn't know why he has become so unpleasant.

When a woman is upset by his going into the cave, instead of giving up the cave, a man can make a few small changes and the problem can be alleviated. He does not need to deny his true needs or reject his masculine nature.

How to Communicate Support to a Venusian

As we have discussed, when a man goes into his cave or becomes quiet he is saying "I need some time to think about this, please stop talking to me. I will be back." He doesn't realize that a woman may hear "I don't love you, I can't stand to listen to you, I am leaving and I am never coming back!" To counteract this message and to give her the correct message he can learn to say the four magic words: "I will be back."

When a man pulls away, a woman appreciates him saying out loud "I need some time to think about this. I will be back" or "I need some time to be alone. I will be back." It is amazing how the simple words "I will be back" make such a profound difference.

Women greatly appreciate this reassurance. When a man understands how important this is to a woman, then he is able to remember to give this reassurance.

If a woman felt abandoned or rejected by her father or if her mother felt rejected by her husband, then she (the child) will be even more sensitive to feeling abandoned. For this reason, she should never be judged for needing this reassurance. Similarly, a man should not be judged for his need for the cave.

A woman should not be judged for needing this reassurance, just as a man should not be judged for needing to withdraw.

When a woman is less wounded by her past and if she understands a man's need to spend time in the cave, then her need for reassurance will be less.

I remember making this point in a seminar and a woman asking, "I am so sensitive to my husband's silence, but as a child I never felt abandoned or rejected. My mother never felt rejected by my father. Even when they got a divorce they did it in a loving way."

Then she laughed. She realized how she had been duped. Then she started to cry. Of course her mother had felt rejected. Of course she had felt rejected. Her parents were divorced! Like her parents, she also had denied their painful feelings.

In an age when divorce is so common, it is even more important that men be sensitive to giving reassurance. Just as men can support women by making little changes, women need to do the same.

How to Communicate Without Blame

A man commonly feels attacked and blamed by a woman's feelings, especially when she is upset and talks about problems. Because he doesn't understand how we are different, he doesn't readily relate to her need to talk about all of her feelings.

He mistakenly assumes she is telling him about her feelings because she thinks he is somehow responsible or to be blamed. Because she is upset and she is talking to him, he assumes she is upset with him. When she complains he hears blame. Many men don't understand the (Venusian) need to share upset feelings with the people they love.

With practice and an awareness of our differences, women can learn how to express their feelings without having them sound like blaming. To reassure a man that he is not being blamed, when a woman expresses her feelings she could pause after a few minutes of sharing and tell him how much she appreciates him for listening.

She could say some of the following comments:

- "I'm sure glad I can talk about it."
- "It sure feels good to talk about it."
- "I'm feeling so relieved that I can talk about this."
- "I'm sure glad I can complain about all this. It makes me feel so much better."
- "Well, now that I've talked about it, I feel much better. Thank you."

This simple change can make a world of difference.

In this same vein, as she describes her problems she can support him by appreciating the things he has done to make her life easier and more fulfilling. For example, if she is complaining about work, occasionally she could mention that it is so nice to have him in her life to come home to; if she is complaining about the house, then she could mention that she appreciates that he fixed the fence; or if she is complaining about finances, mention that she really appreciates how hard he works; or if she is complaining about the frustrations of being a parent, she could mention that she is glad she has his help.

Sharing Responsibility

Good communication requires participation on both sides. A man needs to work at remembering that complaining about problems does not mean blaming and that when a woman complains she is generally just letting go of her frustrations by talking about them. A woman can work at letting him know that though she is complaining she also appreciates him.

For example, my wife just came in and asked how I was doing on this chapter. I said, "I'm almost done. How was your day?"

She said, "Oh, there is so much to do. We hardly have any

time together." The old me would have become defensive and then reminded her of all the time we have spent together, or I would have told her how important it was to meet my deadline. This would have just created tension.

The new me, aware of our differences, understood she was looking for reassurance and understanding and not justifications and explanations. I said, "You're right, we have been really busy. Sit down here on my lap, let me give you a hug. It's been a long day."

She then said, "You feel really good." This was the appreciation I needed in order to be more available to her. She then proceeded to complain more about her day and how exhausted she was. After a few minutes she paused. I then offered to drop off the babysitter so she could relax and meditate before dinner.

She said, "Really, you'll take the babysitter home? That would be great. Thank you!" Again she gave me the appreciation and acceptance I needed to feel like a successful partner, even when she was tired and exhausted.

Women don't think of giving appreciation because they assume a man knows how much she appreciates being heard. He doesn't know. When she is talking about problems, he needs to be reassured that he is still loved and appreciated.

Men feel frustrated by problems unless they are doing something to solve them. By appreciating him, a woman can help him realize that just by listening he is also helping.

A woman does not have to suppress her feelings or even change them to support her partner. She does, however, need to express them in a way that doesn't make him feel attacked, accused, or blamed. Making a few small changes can make a big difference.

Four Magic Words of Support

The four magic words to support a man are "It's not your fault." When a woman is expressing her upset feelings she can support a man by pausing occasionally to encourage him by saying "I really appreciate your listening, and if this sounds as if I'm saying it's your fault, that's not what I mean. It's not your fault."

A woman can learn to be sensitive to her listener when she understands his tendency to start feeling like a failure when he hears a lot of problems.

Just the other day my sister called me and talked about a difficult experience that she was going through. As I listened I kept remembering that to support my sister I didn't have to give her any solutions. She needed someone just to listen. After ten minutes of just listening and occasionally saying things like "uh-huh," "oh," and "really!" she then said, "Well, thank you, John. I feel so much better."

It was much easier to hear her because I knew she was not blaming me. She was blaming someone else. I find it more difficult when my wife is unhappy because it is easier for me to feel blamed. However, when my wife encourages me to listen by appreciating me, it becomes much easier to be a good listener.

What to Do When You Feel Like Blaming

Reassuring a man that it is not his fault or that he is not being blamed works only as long as she truly is not blaming him, disapproving of him, or criticizing him. If she is attacking him, then she should share her feelings with someone else. She should wait until she is more loving and centered to talk to him. She could share her resentful feelings with someone she is not upset with, who will be able to give her the support she needs. Then when she feels more loving and forgiving she can successfully approach him to share her feelings.

How to Listen Without Blaming

A man often blames a woman for being blaming when she is innocently talking about problems. This is very destructive to the relationship because it blocks communication.

Imagine a woman saying, "All we ever do is work, work, work. We don't have any fun anymore. You are so serious." A man could very easily feel she is blaming him.

If he feels blamed, I suggest he not blame back and say "I feel like you are blaming me."

Instead I suggest saying "It is difficult to hear you say I am so serious. Are you saying it is all my fault that we don't have more fun?"

Or he could say "It hurts when I hear you say I am so serious and we don't have any fun. Are you saying that it is all my fault?"

In addition, to improve the communication he can give her a way out. He could say "It feels like you are saying it is all my fault that we work so much. Is that true?"

Or he could say "When you say we don't have any fun and that I am so serious, I feel like you are saying it is all my fault. Are you?"

All of these responses are respectful and give her a chance to take back any blame that he might have felt. When she says "Oh, no, I'm not saying it's all your fault" he will probably feel somewhat relieved.

Another approach that I find most helpful is to remember that she always has a right to be upset and that once she gets it out, she will feel much better. This awareness allows me to relax and remember that if I can listen without taking it personally, then when she needs to complain she will be so appreciative of me. Even if she was blaming me, she will not hold on to it.

The Art of Listening

As a man learns to listen and interpret a woman's feelings correctly, communication becomes easier. As with any art, listening requires practice. Each day when I get home, I will generally seek out Bonnie and ask her about her day, thus practicing this art of listening.

If she is upset or has had a stressful day, at first I will feel that she is saying I am somehow responsible and thus to blame. My greatest challenge is to not take it personally, to not misunderstand her. I do this by constantly reminding myself that we speak different languages. As I continue to ask "What else happened?" I find that there are many other things bothering her. Gradually I start to see that I am not solely responsible for her upset. After a while, when she begins to appreciate me for listening, then, even if I was *partially* responsible for her discomfort, she becomes very grateful, accepting, and loving.

Although listening is an important skill to practice, some days a man is too sensitive or stressed to translate the intended meaning of her phrases. At such times he should not even attempt to listen. Instead he could kindly say "This isn't a good time for me. Let's talk later."

Sometimes a man doesn't realize that he can't listen until she begins talking. If he becomes very frustrated, while listening he should not try to continue—he'll just become increasingly upset. That does not serve him or her. Instead, the respectful thing to say is "I really want to hear what you are saying, but right now it is very difficult for me to listen. I think I need some time to think about what you have just said."

As Bonnie and I have learned to communicate in a way that respects our differences and understand each other's needs, our marriage has become so much easier. I have witnessed this same transformation in thousands of individuals and couples. Relationships thrive when communication reflects a ready acceptance and respect of people's innate differences.

When misunderstandings arise, remember that we speak different languages; take the time necessary to translate what your partner really means or wants to say. This definitely takes practice, but it is well worth it.

5

Speaking Different Languages

*A*fter men read my books or watch the videos of my seminars, many of them comment on one thing. For them, the most helpful insight involves discovering how women communicate for different reasons than men do. It sometimes seems that we are speaking different languages.

Women use language, just like men do, to make points and solve problems. However, they also use talking as a way of discovering what they want to say; and sometimes they talk about their feelings in order to sort things out, as a means toward eventually feeling better. At other times, women feel a need to share and express their feelings, simply as a means to get closer, to experience greater intimacy.

Men don't instinctively understand these various approaches, because men tend to use language primarily as a way of making points. When men talk about problems, they are generally looking for solutions. A man mistakenly assumes that when a woman talks about her feelings and problems his role as listener is to efficiently assist her in feeling better by offering her solutions. Like a fireman in an emergency situation, he is impatient to get to the fire and put it out as quickly as possible. When she is upset, he wants to put out the fire of her feelings by giving solutions.

> **When she is upset, he wants to put out the fire of her feelings by giving solutions.**

Learning to listen *patiently*—and not just *passively*—is a new skill for men. Yet repeatedly men report that keeping quiet and resisting the strong tendency to interrupt a woman with solutions has dramatically improved their relationships. Their partners are much happier and appreciative. Lucky is the man who discovers that satisfying a woman's need to communicate and be heard is the most important requirement in making relationships loving and harmonious. When a man is a good listener, a woman can repeatedly find the place in her heart that is capable of loving him and embracing him just the way he is.

Making It Easy to Communicate

Art said, "I could never figure out why Lindsay would talk so much about the same problems, particularly when there was nothing I could do about them. It was a relief to know that I am not expected to solve her problems. It made it so easy to communicate. If I could just listen and not have to solve her problems to make her feel better, then okay—I could do that.

> **After a long day of solving problems, the last thing I want to do is come home to another list of problems I have to solve.**

"After a long day of solving problems, the last thing I want to do is come home to another list of problems I have to solve. When she would talk about problems, I always thought I would have to do more before I could relax. Now I just listen and relax, knowing that for her to feel better she basically needs to feel heard."

Saying the Wrong Thing

Les learned to restrain his impulse to respond. "When Gloria talked about her day with the kids, whatever I said was the wrong thing. She would feel misunderstood, unappreciated, and attacked. I couldn't figure it out. She was the one who wanted to have more conversations, but every time we talked we would end up feeling frustrated. She complained that I didn't listen, but every time I said something it made it worse.

"I learned just not to say anything. After a while, when she would talk, I would just begin to space out. I would get really bored and tired. It all sounded the same and I just wasn't interested. When she read *Mars and Venus Together Forever,* everything started to change.

> **She told me she really appreciated me listening to her talk about her feelings and that I really didn't have to say anything.**

"She told me that she really appreciated being able to share her feelings and understood that it must be hard for me just to listen, particularly since she didn't want me to offer her solutions. She went on to let me know that if I just listened and didn't say anything it would still be helpful.

"Now I don't say anything. Knowing that I am helping her makes a big difference. I like it when she says, 'Thanks for listening—it really helps.' It's different now that I know I am giving her what she needs by just listening. I am slowly starting to connect more and be more aware of her life, and be interested. I've learned I don't have to solve her problems and she will feel better. Now we both look forward to being together. She feels I love her and I get to be helpful."

A Blueprint for Relationships

Danny understood why he and his wife argued. "We had been married for fourteen years. We loved each other but we would argue all the time. I thought Marsha was just being too negative. After a few years of counseling, we called it quits and separated. Then I read *Men Are from Mars*. For me, it was literally out of left field to hear that women needed to talk about their feelings and problems before they could get on to feeling happier and more loving.

> It was literally out of left field to hear that women needed to talk about their feelings before they could get on to feeling happier and more loving.

"I had always viewed her 'feelings' as an unreasonable attempt to criticize me. Her feelings made me feel like she didn't appreciate anything I did. Learning about Venusians and their valid need to talk freed me to not take it so personally. I realized that I had been the negative one. She was just sharing her feelings and I was having a negative reaction. This then caused us to spiral downward, saying mean things about each other.

"I called her up and told her what I was learning. She was interested and we went out to dinner. It was great, suddenly we were agreeing. We had words to express our feelings and positive ways of supporting each other. Before, it was not that we didn't love each other, but that we couldn't communicate in a positive manner. I really wasn't listening.

"Now I use *Men Are from Mars* as a blueprint for our relationship. You can't build a house without a plan. I think I just gave up because I didn't know what to do. Now I have the plan to build our relationship. I want to thank you so much. You have given me back the most precious thing in my life."

Learning the Customs on Venus

Martha had comments to make on listening. "Recognizing that it was difficult for men to be great listeners helped me appreciate Roger's attempts at listening. Instead of feeling that he didn't care enough to listen, I now know that when he does give solutions, it is not that he doesn't care but that he has forgotten what I need.

> When he gives solutions, it is not that he doesn't care but that he has forgotten what I need.

"He is from Mars and is still learning the customs on Venus. Old habits take time to change. Instead of giving him a hard time, I just smile and say, 'I just need to be real Venusian right now, you don't have to say anything.' He doesn't get defensive but instead smiles and says, 'Oops.' And that's it. I go on and he listens."

He Apologized for Being So Insensitive

Margaret said, "When I would talk about things that bother me, Tom would say either 'What's the point?' or 'Don't start!' It would shut me down. After a while I just stopped liking him. After reading your book, he apologized for being so insensitive. He told me that he wanted to start listening and that he wouldn't cut me off. Wow! Everything changed. Now I really look forward to spending time with him. Not only do I love him, but I like him as well."

I Didn't Just Want Lip Service

Jessica had this story: "When I first heard John Gray talk about this, I didn't like it. The last thing I wanted was a man to listen to me if he didn't want to. I wanted a man to *want* to listen to me; I didn't just want lip service. I wanted a man who cared enough and really was interested in what I had to say. It seemed degrading to ask a man to listen when I could sense that he didn't want to. The thought of him occasionally nodding his head and mechanically saying, 'um-hum . . . um-hum . . . um-hum . . . really," was not my idea of intimacy. But I tried it and I was amazed—I did feel better.

> **I didn't want a man to listen
> if he didn't really want to.**

"I liked being able to talk without being interrupted. It had never happened before. No finishing my sentences, no solutions, no defensive comments. It was great. Now instead of feeling that he doesn't want to listen, I know that he is willing to listen because he wants to help. He may not really *want* to listen, but he does *want* to help and for that I really feel loved!"

She Had the Problem, Not Me

Steve discussed his learning process. "Whenever I would get together with my ex-wife it was trouble. She said she couldn't talk with me. That was fine with me but we shared two wonderful children. It was tearing them apart to see their parents rejecting and resenting each other.

"I didn't have a problem communicating but she did. After all, she was the one who wouldn't talk to me and I was a lawyer, a professional counselor. It was clear that I could put my feelings to the side and talk rationally. She had the problem, not me.

"I finally realized that if she didn't want to talk to me, then I must be a part of the problem. Using my legal interrogation skills, I was putting her on trial each time we talked. When she would share her feelings, I would interrupt repeatedly and correct her. I would explain away the reasons she felt upset about things. I would repeatedly invalidate her generalizations with counterexamples, without any consideration of her feelings.

I was putting her on trial each time we talked.

"After reading your book, I wrote her a letter and apologized for being inconsiderate and told her that in the future I would try very hard to listen in a respectful way without making put-down comments. This one comment and realization transformed our whole relationship. I learned to leave my legal skills in the office and with her to just listen and try to understand the validity of her point of view—even if I disagreed. Now we are not only talking, but we are friends. Our children see their parents as loving and respectful of each other. What a special gift this message is."

I Don't Need to Be Fixed

Erica said, "Each time we argued about something, after a while we would end up arguing about the way we were arguing. He would say it was my problem that I was so unhappy and that if I would just live in the moment and appreciate what was good in my life, then I would feel much better. Then I wouldn't make such a big deal of things.

"I would say that he didn't understand, that he didn't care, and that it wasn't all my problem. I told him I couldn't talk with him if he kept trying to fix me. I needed him to share with me the responsibility for our problems and see the validity of my side.

"It's okay if we disagree. I just need you to hear and understand my point of view."

"By understanding that men automatically want to solve problems, I was able to change my approach. Now, when we start to argue, it diffuses the tension when I first pause and then prepare him for what I want to say.

"I say, 'You don't have to agree with me. That's okay. I just need you to hear and understand my point of view. We don't have to solve this problem right away. If you just listen to me, then I can also hear what you have to say. That will make me feel much better.'

"When I do this he suddenly calms down and listens. We don't have to fight. He gets to be right and I get the right to share and express how I feel—without being interrupted, corrected, or fixed."

You Don't Understand

Paul shared, "My wife used to always complain, 'You don't understand!' She still does sometimes, but now it doesn't turn into an argument. Before we took your workshop, when she said I didn't understand I would argue and explain that I did. Sometimes I would even explain I understood what was bothering her better than she did. This definitely didn't work.

"One simple change made a world of difference. Now, when she says that I don't understand, I realize she is really saying that *she* needs to tell me more before I can fully understand. I have learned to say in response, 'Okay, you're right. I don't understand, tell me more.' This one change has stopped all our arguments.

> **"Okay, you're right. I don't understand, tell me more." This one change has stopped all our arguments.**

"I have learned that when she has a chance to keep talking without my interrupting, inevitably she becomes more loving toward me. Although it takes a little more time than I would like, she does eventually feel more understood.

"It was hard for me to acknowledge that I didn't understand her, particularly when I thought I did. But I finally learned that when she doesn't feel understood, then I am definitely not understanding her in the way she needs. Simply to agree that I don't understand was really giving her the understanding she needed. To say she was right, and agree that I didn't understand, was in effect saying that I did understand that she doesn't feel understood. With this support she could then continue to share and explore what else she was feeling. My acknowledging that I didn't understand actually helped her to feel understood."

Giving Up Anger and Getting What I Needed

Jerry related his story. "The other day my wife was very concerned about some problems I was having at work. Normally I would have gotten very angry that she was giving me advice, doubting me, and really treading on my territory. Instead of getting angry, I practiced dodging and tried to not take her comments and fears personally.

> **Instead of getting angry, I practiced not taking her comments and fears personally.**

"I just let her talk and didn't get angry. I realized she was from Venus and her way of dealing with her fears was to talk about them. After giving her what she needed, I then asked her for what *I* needed: when she was done I said, 'I know you are afraid and it's important to talk about that. What I need to hear from you is that you trust me to take care of things and that you're glad that I'm here to handle things.'

"Having felt heard, she was able to then give me the support I needed. She very willingly said she trusted me and was so grateful we were together. I smiled and felt good as I hugged her, instead of feeling beaten down by her fears and feelings."

Alarm Signals

Sam shared his insights. "I have learned that when Tia acts in a cordial way but doesn't talk much, it is an alarm signal. It means something is brewing inside and if I don't get her to talk soon, it will just grow worse. When she seems distant, instead of just ignoring her I take notice. There is generally something that I've done or neglected to do. and it is building up inside her and preventing her from being loving.

> **When she seems distant, instead of just ignoring her I take notice.**

"If I don't notice that she is upset, she feels that I don't care. And if she has to finally initiate a conversation to express her feelings, then she is much more upset and it takes a lot longer to get things resolved. My willingness to notice and ask her what's the matter goes a long way to resolve whatever feelings that are building up inside."

Going Fishing

Harvey tuned in to his wife's needs. "When Rebecca wants to talk the most, she acts like she doesn't even want to talk. Then, when I start a conversation, she'll start out saying there's not much to talk about.

"I say, 'Is something the matter?' and she says it's nothing. I used to just walk away thinking I had done my duty and now I could watch some TV. That was a big mistake.

"Now I've learned not to take her literally. When she says there's not much to talk about, I now hear that she wants to talk but needs me to ask her questions to gradually draw her out. Instead of walking away, I go fishing. I keep asking her questions until I get a bite.

> **Instead of walking away, I go fishing. I keep asking her questions until I get a bite.**

"She doesn't just want me to listen, she wants me to notice that she probably needs to talk. She wants me to be tuned in to what's happening in her life, so that I already have a sense of why she is upset. She wants me to ask her questions that reveal that I know what is going on in her life. Just as when you're fishing, it takes patience, but eventually I ask the right question and she begins to open up.

"I used to think that if she wanted to talk about something, then she should just come out and say it. That's how I am. But I am starting to understand that for Venusians it's a comforting feeling that someone cares and is watching out for them. I like being that guy."

I Listen Because I Love You

Wendy said, "The thing I love most about Gerald is his willingness to listen. When there is a problem we talk about it. Even though it would be much easier to gloss over it and watch TV, he is willing to sit down and listen. What I have to say sometimes is definitely not very nice, nor is it to the point. He doesn't always agree, nor is it very comfortable, but he does it anyway."

Gerald responded, "She sure is right about that. It's hard to hear her feelings; a part of me wants to run, but I stay because I have learned how important it is to her. Although I don't necessarily like what she is saying, I listen because I love her and I know she needs this support from me.

> It's hard to hear her feelings; a part of me wants
> to run, but I stay because I have learned how
> important it is to her.

"I even say to her, 'This is very difficult for me but I am willing to listen and consider your feelings because I love you.' Saying it out loud not only helps her feel my willingness to listen but makes it easier for me too. I suppose it helps me to remember once again that love is the answer and by listening I am giving her the love she needs. In the most effective way, I am doing what she needs most from me."

Anger Erupts When We Try to Talk

Bruce told his story. "We have been married for twenty years. It is a second marriage for both of us. We brought two families together—I brought three kids and she brought one. We raised all four children. We have had difficult communication problems since early in our marriage. There has been a great deal of mistrust and defensiveness. After the kids left, our marriage got worse and we semi-separated for a while. We have had separate bedrooms for years. A great deal of anger and resentment erupts when we try to talk, even about little things.

"When I read through your book, I saw things that sounded like what Gretchen had been saying to me for years. I had really never understood what she was talking about, or why it was such a big thing. I also saw stuff I had been trying to tell her, to no avail. I saw explanations for things I was experiencing but had not been able to visualize in a positive perspective. The hope for finally being able to communicate was exciting to me.

"Gretchen, however, was not so enthusiastic. Her response to me was: I will believe it when I see it. If you change, I will consider these ideas. Instead of getting defensive in response to her mistrust, I realized the validity of her feelings. After years of her feeling neglected, I am finding it takes time to heal and re-build trust. I am also finding that my gentle persistence in car-ing enough to make changes and in learning how to listen is helping her to let go of her resistance, and is helping me too. It is not easy to start over and have your every step mistrusted and resisted. However, I am feeling stronger in the process, and I like that feeling.

> **My gentle persistence was just what she needed to help her to let go of her resistance.**

"When it doesn't seem to be working, instead of dumping my angry feelings on Gretchen, I start privately writing out and venting my feelings in a 'love letter,' as you suggest in your books. I start out feeling very angry and upset and end up feeling that I have achieved a release and begin to experi-ence loving feelings again. These loving feelings help me to understand her perspective, and once again I try to be a bet-ter listener.

"My wife and I have had tender moments and brief periods of meaningful communication. However, we still sometimes keep our distance and keep our guard up. Even though we have a lot of negative history, there is hope. I have become much more excited about my life and for the possibilities within life.

"I can see more clearly now the problems in our relation-ship and I know what to do. I can see changes within me where I feel more loving of myself, of my wife, and of others. New people have been coming into my life and old friends have been returning. There is a new dimension to life that feels won-derful.

"Gretchen and I still upset each other. In such cases, I used to say, 'Oh no, not this again! I wish she would some-how learn how to flow with life and get off my case!' Now I am getting to where I can say, 'Well, there is something more I need to learn. I am upset now and I know how to take care of it. I can go out and write a love letter or I can take some time to go for a walk and think things through a bit and calm down.'

"Although I don't enjoy getting upset and having to process these feelings, I always seem to get new insights about myself and my wife. As a result I am learning to be easier on myself and I hope on Gretchen as well. Through understanding in a positive way why we have been misunderstanding each other, I have found hope again. This has been an incredible journey."

Feeling Better About Myself

Renata shared, "Learning about our differences helped me feel better about myself as well. On the way home from a vacation in South Carolina, I began thinking out loud, stating what I had to do when I returned home the next week—and the next month, the next three months, and so on.

"I finished my sentence with, 'Yes, and in six months I have to go to the dentist.' Then what John Gray said regarding how women think came back to my mind—not only out loud but expanding outward too. He has made it all right for me to be the way I am.

"I have four sons, and they used to criticize me for thinking out loud—they accused me of 'babbling.' But now I know I'm just being Venusian and thinking out loud."

Our Marriage Was Okay but Lacked Excitement

Ian described how he and his wife improved their communication. "Ten years ago Ellen wanted to take off on a romantic weekend. I was very much in love with my wife, but I'd been noticing a kind of sameness to our life—our sex, communication, dealings with our children. The marriage was okay, but there was a lack of excitement. It just seemed to me that the relationship wasn't being nurtured. There was love there—always—and commitment, no question. I knew I was going to remain married to Ellen for the rest of my life. Everything else was booming—business, and the kids—but in the marriage something had gone flat. My commitment was there, but from an emotional standpoint I felt that the tank was becoming empty.

"So I persuaded Ellen to give up on the vacation idea and go to a John Gray seminar. And in the first five minutes I knew we were in the right place. He started by talking about all the mistakes *he* had made in his relationships, and right away I felt a tremendous weight lift off my shoulders. I didn't have to be a perfect person! I didn't have to be responsible for making the relationship perfect, for creating our happiness. In the first two minutes, John's openness and self-disclosure made me feel right.

"And in the longer run, I gained an emotional language. My spiritual side was developed. My physical side was strong—I was a P.E. teacher. But I didn't really have an emotional language, and there were feelings I had that I was never able to describe or express.

"Certain kinds of communication had always been threatening to my sense of power as a man. I was vulnerable, afraid to express disappointments and unhappiness, because I thought that letting on that I felt such things would jeopardize the whole relationship. I thought I had to always have a solution for everything and be in complete control. I had to be a strong man for this marriage, didn't I?

> **I thought I had to always have a solution for everything and be in complete control.**

"But, to my amazement, with the communication tools John taught, everything just opened up and I felt a connection with my own self. I felt a tremendous burden disappear and insights began pouring into me from all levels. I felt freer than I had in a long, long time; I felt love for myself and for my wife beginning to flow again. And I felt a tremendous feeling of hope.

"What accounted for this great flow of feeling? I could finally give voice to feelings that I had never expressed before. I learned to first give Ellen a chance to talk. I stopped getting caught up in trying to change how she felt. I gave up trying to give solutions all the time. Instead I would listen and then, when she was done, I could share my thoughts, feelings, and experiences and she would listen.

"In a practical sense, the impact of that seminar—a permanent impact—was that when my wife and I argued we could come back to a balance point a lot more quickly than before. I wouldn't shut down for as long as I had—my pattern before had been to brood and be moody and go on and on with it. Now, the time I spent doing that dramatically decreased. With John's techniques, I could come back to a balanced, loving space without a fear of 'confrontation.'"

My pattern before had been to brood and be moody and go on and on with it.

"For example, if Ellen was doing something that bothered me, I would be able to tell her—rather than shoving those feelings down or (as in the past) raising my voice, trying to be more controlling with anger, and just blurting things out. This new avenue was more respectful, and involved listening both to Ellen's side and to *my* own voice inside.

"Once this became habit, it was obvious that these new communication skills actually worked. They provided me with a road map to guide myself on an emotional level. I could always do that on a physical, intellectual, and professional level, but now I had a path to the emotional level as well.

"*Everything* was affected. We became so much closer, the communication opened tenfold, and our sex life was enlivened to the point it had been in the beginning—and this continues today. But perhaps the most surprising impact of my new listening skills and understanding of gender differences came in my relationships with our son and daughter.

"Because I was more forgiving of myself and the mistakes I had made as a man and a parent, I became more patient with them, more compassionate, more supportive. Because I was now supporting myself and my spouse emotionally, I could do that with my children as well. Before that, I had taken a more dictatorial approach with them, though there was always love underneath. So, consequently, my children are very expressive with their own emotions and comfortable around peers and adults—more comfortable than I ever was. It's tremendously satisfying to see them getting the benefit of *my* own benefits from this work.

> **As a parent I became more patient,**
> **compassionate, and supportive.**

"We have regular family meetings, and if a conflict arises, we now have ways of working things out. Based on John's techniques of listening, everybody gets heard. Anyone at any time can call a family meeting to express thoughts, and the children do that. They thrive on it, actually.

"So, you see, we have something to give them: our ways of communicating are our true gifts to our children. They see us communicating and growing, arguing but making up and apologizing, committed to each other to make it work, and hearing each other out. We know that every time we give to each other we are also giving to our children."

Love at First Sight

Ellen told her side. "It began twenty years ago. I was only twenty-four, and I had known this man for three weeks and decided I wanted to marry him. Three months later we were married.

"We were very similar, really. Ian's parents had divorced when he was fourteen, and my father had died when I was eleven. So we were both raised by single parents.

"For the first three years, we had lots of fun. We had our kids, and seven years later after we married, by year ten, we weren't having sex a lot, and I was feeling a lot of anger. There just wasn't a lot of aliveness in our relationship, even though we were committed to it.

> **By year ten, we weren't having sex a lot, and**
> **I was feeling a lot of anger.**

"Ian decided we needed to take a seminar from John Gray. Actually, I was afraid. I thought we might realize that we'd chosen the wrong mates, that I'd find I didn't love Ian or that he didn't love me.

"What happened was a total catharsis. We learned the tools that enabled us to be in this relationship. The main tool for me as a woman was to become more vulnerable. I saw there that I was on the masculine side of life—always focused on solving everyone else's problems and ignoring my own needs and feelings. John showed us the way a woman needed to talk, talk, talk. And how that was the natural way for a woman.

"Second, and almost more personally profound for me, at that seminar I had a huge breakdown around my feelings of loss for my father. I had never experienced these feelings, but I began to cry about them, and John saw me crying and called me up to the front of the room. He asked me if I'd like to share my feelings, and this progressed into a catharsis about having felt abandoned by men, not being able to trust men, and feeling that I could not dare to be vulnerable to men. John called Ian up to hold me when I expressed my feelings about my father. Allowing Ian to be there to witness this was just an incredible experience for me!

"If we women could just *trust*, and teach men *not to try to fix but just to listen,* then our hearts would automatically open up and we would feel much closer to the men. This is what happened to me. That experience improved our whole relationship: our physical life, our intimacy, our relationship with the children. We stopped putting the children in the middle in order to keep our distance from each other.

....
We have the tools to express our needs, feelings, likes, dislikes, and the format not to get hooked, not to take things so personally.
....

"Without John's seminar, I don't know where we would be. With it, though, we are life partners. We have the tools to express our needs, feelings, likes, dislikes, and the format not to get hooked, not to take things so personally. The format allows us, out of love, to be able to hear each other and try to support each other in what we are asking for and feeling.

"How do we make each other happy? Both of us try to keep the romance alive. We prioritize working on our relationship by taking time to have fun together. We take time away from the kids to be romantic and we take time away from each other to do things on our own. When we come back together, we are missing one another and have more to share.

"As for what I do for Ian to make him happy, well, he needs to be trusted—so I back off from giving him advice and suggestions unless he really asks. I try to appreciate him as much as I can for everything he does.

"What does Ian do to make me happy? He listens. He does caring little things for me. He brings me a cup of tea every morning. He participates greatly in the parenting. But the biggest thing is his incredible respect for me. He praises me and expects our children to act the same way. Those are the ways we make each other happy."

Talkers and Thinkers

This is Suzanne's story. "I am forty-seven years old and have been married for ten years. My husband, Rich, and I have known each other for twelve years and have no children.

"During the first several years of our marriage, I felt that there was not enough communication between us. I'm the 'talker' and Rich is the 'thinker' in the family.

"I would try and try to get him to open up and share his thoughts and feelings with me, but to no avail. I came from a previous marriage where there was no communication, and I was determined that this marriage was going to be different— or it would surely fail as well.

"Like many couples, we didn't know how to express ourselves. Rich didn't know how to verbalize what he felt, and I didn't know what words to use to get him to open up. I found myself getting more and more angry and frustrated; the laughter had gone out of our marriage.

> **As soon as I would begin to speak, I could see him shut down and become defensive.**

"I would watch *Oprah* and get ideas on how to communicate better; then I would try to explain the techniques to Rich when he came home. As soon as I would begin to speak, I could see him shut down and become defensive. His defensiveness was extremely difficult for me to deal with. An argument would ensue. He would then make a small effort to be better for about a week or two and then we'd be right back where we started.

"My main concern, besides Rich's defensiveness, was that I was feeling taken advantage of and not being 'taken care of.' I wanted a man in my life who would take control once in a while. It seemed I was the one running the household, doing all the chores, doing all the worrying, and not even receiving so much as a thank-you for my efforts. My resentment was really beginning to build up. Rich always had clean underwear in his drawer and fresh shirts in his closet. Why couldn't I open my drawer and closet to find my clothes ready to wear? I found myself falling out of love with my husband and didn't know where to turn.

"A disturbing habit was forming. Every few weeks, when it all became too much, I would attempt to explain to him what I was feeling, but all I would do was cry. He would promise to do more around the house; again, it only lasted a week or so.

"Then I heard about your book, *Men Are from Mars, Women Are from Venus*. I was reading the book when I heard you were speaking in New York City. I asked Rich if he would go, and he did. It was the best thing that could have happened for us!

"As you spoke, he heard *my* words coming out of *your* mouth. He saw us in everything you were saying. The most important thing you spoke about was what really turns women on—taking out the trash, washing the dishes, folding the laundry, etc. Rich was amazed at that; I suppose a lot of men are. We talked about it on the way home, and since that night our relationship has not been the same.

> As you spoke, he heard *my* words coming out of *your* mouth. He saw us in everything you were saying.

"Now, without being asked, Rich takes out the trash, takes the recycling to the curb, washes dishes, folds laundry, vacuums, handles all the bills, etc., etc. And I thank him when he does these things for me.

"We keep communications open, but it takes work . . . it doesn't always happen spontaneously. He takes the time to listen to me, even when it is not what he wants to be doing. If I read Rich's face and can tell there is something on his mind, or I may have said something he didn't like, I encourage him to tell me what he's thinking. If he doesn't want to talk, then I don't press. I think, however, that because he doesn't feel pressured he is much more willing to share what's going on.

> **I encourage him to tell me what he's thinking. If he doesn't want to talk, then I don't press.**

"We tell each other 'I love you' every day. We don't leave the house or arrive home without kissing each other hello or good-bye. One thing Rich has always done since I met him is to call me at least once a day, just to see how I'm doing, and he always tells me when I can expect him home.

"This brings to mind something that happened the other day. I was baking cookies for Christmas and accidentally put in twice the amount of baking soda the recipe called for. I began baking, and the first batch of cookies tasted salty. I had to throw out the entire batch of dough and start all over again. Naturally, I didn't have enough ingredients to make another batch, so I had to run to the store.

"Before leaving, I asked Rich if he would help me when I returned, and he said, 'Why don't you do it tomorrow?' That's not the answer I was looking for. I said nothing, and went to the store. When I returned ten minutes later, he must have given some thought to what he said to me, because he met me at the door and said, 'I'll help you. Just tell me what you want me to do.'

"A feeling of total happiness came over me. Two years ago, he would have sat in his recliner while I baked the second batch.

> **Two years ago, he would have sat in his recliner while I baked the second batch.**

"As I said before, it takes constant work. Bad habits die hard. What makes me so happy is that now both of us really work at making the other happy. If we unintentionally say or do something that may make the other sad or angry, we acknowledge that we were wrong, apologize, and make it right.

"We're the happiest we've ever been, and it keeps getting better."

6

Men Are Still from Mars, Women Are Still from Venus

*I*n my relationship seminars, I explain that the differences between men and women make it seem as if we are from different planets.

While thousands of people nod their heads in agreement when I give my examples, there are some who don't fully relate. In fact, it is not at all uncommon for many women to say that they more fully relate to my examples of being a man. They feel that they are from Mars and not Venus. I assure them that nothing is wrong, and that even though society has to a great extent influenced them to become more masculine, they are still from Venus.

There are many factors that influence a woman having a more developed masculine side or a man having a more developed feminine side. Quite commonly, if a girl bonds more closely with her father or if she was raised in a very male-dominated household, she will tend to more fully develop her masculine side. Likewise, if a boy bonds more closely with his mother or if he is raised in a very female-dominated household, he will tend to more fully develop his female side.

Generally speaking, though, a woman becomes more masculine when she has not witnessed a woman being feminine and also being respected. Likewise, a man becomes more feminine when he has not witnessed a man being loving and also being strong and powerful.

Cultural backgrounds and certain ethnic groups also have characteristics that are more "masculine" or "feminine." For example, Germans and Swedes tend to frown upon open displays of emotion or talking just for the sake of talking instead of trying to make a point, whereas Italian families are much more emotionally expressive.

Sometimes the different feminine tendencies don't show up in a woman because when she is single and rather isolated, she has become the Martian and takes care of herself. Once she is in a relationship, many traditional female tendencies begin to emerge.

In other cases, a woman will become more masculine or Martian because in her relationship over time she experiences that it is not safe to be feminine.

For example, the feminine need to talk more may cause too much frustration or make her look weak. Rather than appear too needy or cause conflict, she automatically begins to suppress her feminine side.

Men sometimes also feel that they are from Venus. Creative men in particular experience both their male and female sides. These men generally are attracted to women who are more on their male side. Again, the formula holds true: differences attract.

In some cases, these men didn't have positive role models for expressing masculine power. They do not know how to assert themselves and set limits, but also be loving and caring. To fulfill the woman, they are willing to sacrifice their needs. Not only are they personally weakened, but when they become more feminine, women lose their attraction to them and leave. By using new relationship skills, these men can automatically begin to develop their masculine sides while also respecting their feminine sides.

When a Man Is on His Female Side

When a man is operating too much from his female side, the antidote is for him to do things that will immediately allow his mate to nurture his male side. He should look to her for appreciation and acknowledgment. When she supports him in this way, and he can more quickly reestablish balance, she benefits as well.

If a man is on his female side, applying new relationship skills may not at first feel natural. His female side will say "Why do I have to duck and dodge and make it safe for her? I want her to make it safe for me! I want to talk too."

By overcoming this resistance and learning to listen first and "contain" before expressing his own feelings, a man exercises and strengthens his male side. When his male side has successfully supported her female side, it is then productive and healthy for him to allow her to be there for his female side. After he has nurtured her female side and she has nurtured his masculine side by appreciating his support, then it is fine for him to look freely to her to nurture his female side.

If a man has a more developed female side, he will feel a pull to be nurtured by his mate's masculine side. He will feel a greater need for her to be there for him. He will get upset when she doesn't want to talk or work on the relationship. He will complain that she is not there for him in the relationship. He will ask lots of questions to get her to talk more. He will want her to listen and understand his feelings and offer sympathy and help him in various ways.

A man's female side has legitimate needs, but to allow them full access in a relationship will tend to push a woman to her masculine side. Such a man can better support the needs of his feminine side by going to a men's support group, spending more time with his male friends, doing personal growth work, or looking to God for this kind of support.

Requiring his partner to support his female side puts an enormous strain on the relationship.

....
A woman is already needing more support to connect with her female side; she can't find her female side and also be the man for his female side.
....

When a man looks to a woman primarily for this kind of support, not only does he push her to her masculine side but it may even weaken him. Unable to talk with other males about their problems, many men complain to their wives. This creates even greater imbalance.

After a while, as he talks more and more she will talk less and less. A man needs to be careful not to "whine" too much with his wife or she will begin mothering and her desire for him will flicker and dim. As a general suggestion, a man should not express more sensitivities than his mate. If he is more sensitive, he will need to toughen up a bit by nurturing his male side more.

When a woman says she wants a sensitive man, she really means that she wants a man who is strong but is sensitive to her needs. Quite commonly, women are turned off when a man becomes more sensitive than she is. Briefly, in the beginning, it may seem very attractive, particularly if she is on her male side, but very quickly, if it persists for too long, she becomes increasingly annoyed.

A man needs to be careful not to look to a woman to fulfill his feminine needs. Ideally, a man should look to a woman primarily to nurture his male side and not his female side. His male side is nurtured every time he feels appreciated, accepted, and trusted. The more nurtured he feels, the stronger and tougher he will be, but at the same time he will grow more sensitive to her needs. This strength and sensitivity to her needs is what women really appreciate, and it makes him feel both strong and loving.

If he happens to be more sensitive than she is, it may take a few years to balance out and find his masculine strength in the relationship. In the meantime, he should not burden her with his sensitivities. For example, if his feelings are hurt or if he feels more emotionally needy, he should then talk with men friends and not look to her primarily to support his need to talk and share feelings.

A man achieves balance in a relationship primarily through successfully supporting the female. When a man succeeds in supporting her, then to a great extent his own female side is automatically nurtured. When she is happy, he feels happy because indirectly his own female side is automatically supported. When a man loves a woman and feels a deep connection with her, it is then as though her female side becomes his. Through fulfilling her female side not only is his male side appreciated but his female side is also nurtured.

When a Woman Is on Her Male Side

When a woman feels responsible to nurture a man's female side, it actually puts her out of balance. For example, when he expects her to listen more to his feelings, it has the effect of turning her off not only to him but to her own female side. Automatically, she begins to become more masculine. New relationship skills are required to assist women in returning to their female side.

A woman feels most nurtured when her female side is directly supported. A woman achieves balance through successfully supporting her male partner in supporting her. If she can create a climate in which to receive the support she needs in order to be happy, her male side is also simultaneously developed.

In this way a woman is able to assert her male side to solve the problems while safeguarding her female side through being directly nurtured by her partner. On the other hand, when she directly supports her male partner's female side, she overlooks her own, until one day she wakes up angry and resentful that their caring and understanding are no longer reciprocal.

When a woman is too much on her male side, the antidote

is creating relationships in which her female side blossoms. If she works in a traditionally male role all day, she will have to make deliberate efforts to overcome much inner resistance in order to do this.

When a woman on her masculine side gets home, she may want to go to her cave. She is definitely not in a communicative mood. She feels a much greater need for space than her man does. She needs to solve problems and can't waste time talking about them.

Since her male side wants to be appreciated, accepted, and trusted, she resents it when her partner gives her advice or doesn't recognize all that she does. In most cases, she would rather do things herself. She definitely feels that her partner isn't giving her the appreciation she deserves as a provider.

To support her male side she needs to spend time with other women who can nurture her male side's need to be appreciated.

Ideally, a woman should look to the man in her life for caring, understanding, and respect. These qualities of love nurture her female side. As she gets those needs fulfilled and her appreciation for her partner increases, then she can expect that he will overflow and appreciate all that she does as well.

> **It is definitely not healthy for a woman and man to compete for appreciation in a relationship.**

While it is important for women to be appreciated, they should look to their male partners to support their female sides. Women today need a man's support more than ever to be able to return to their feminine sides at the end of the day.

Emotional Role Reversal and Attraction

With so many women in the workforce, it is becoming more common for them to begin a relationship in emotional role reversal. By pursuing him more actively, a woman causes a man to move more to his female side. Rather than feel a responsibility to initiate a relationship, he waits and lets her do the pursuing.

When a woman is on her male side, she tends to be attracted to a man on his female side and vice versa. Many men sense this automatically and move to their female side. This is a trap. Unless men consciously work to find balance, they will eventually lose their appeal.

When a woman is more masculine, a man tends to become more feminine. Likewise, if a man becomes more feminine, a woman becomes more masculine. If she doesn't learn skills to assist him in nurturing her female side, she will become even more masculine. The more masculine she becomes, the more feminine he becomes.

If a very masculine man becomes more feminine, he is moving toward balance. But if he is already too much on his female side, pushing him farther into it creates greater imbalance.

If he is very feminine and she is very masculine, maintaining attraction requires his slowly but surely developing his masculine side as she develops her feminine side. By developing the male and female sides in tandem, new relationship skills promote greater balance and attraction.

Conventional Relationships

In more conventional relationships, the man is more masculine and the woman is more feminine. The attraction lessens over time if the woman repeatedly experiences that she cannot be supported on her female side. Rather than risk the pain of repeated invalidation or rejection, she closes up and becomes in certain ways more masculine.

The same is true for men. Rather than continuing to do masculine things like make decisions, initiate sex, and solve problems for her, when he doesn't feel appreciated he suppresses his male side. In various ways he will automatically become more feminine. Without the sexual polarity, the attraction between partners dissipates.

Although couples may start out very masculine and feminine, over time they begin to reverse roles emotionally. When a man doesn't feel his masculine side being supported, he then automatically begins to go out of balance. Likewise, when a woman doesn't get the support she needs at the office and at home to be feminine, then she also goes out of balance.

Balancing the Masculine and the Feminine

Ironically, men go out of balance because they are not getting the support from women that they used to get in the old days, while women go out of balance because they are not getting a new kind of support from men.

To solve our modern problems, women need to find within themselves the feminine love they used to share, but without giving up the new power they are expressing. A modern man's challenge is to draw upon his ancient courage and risk failure by trying out new formulas for success in order to support the woman he loves in new ways.

When men and women are unaware of the necessary techniques needed to create balance, emotional role reversal automatically kicks in. For both sexes, it commonly happens in distinct stages.

Emotional Role Reversal and Doing It All

When a woman returns home from work, her tendency is to stay in her masculine side, particularly if there is more work to be done. Instead of relaxing and talking about her problems, she feels that she faces a new list of problems *that need to be solved.*

She either talks about them to get her partner's help to solve them or she doesn't want to talk at all. She feels she has to do it all. To cope with her frustration, she too may begin to withdraw from the relationship and feel a need to go to her cave.

Her experience changes when she is on her female side. When a woman is connected to her feminine side, she is capable of enjoying and appreciating the small details of living. She may be aware of problems, but she does not have to solve them immediately in order to feel good.

When she is too much on her male side, she then suddenly feels an urgency to solve all of life's little and big problems. She feels too responsible for doing "everything" and taking care of everyone. She feels overwhelmed. Instead of feeling loving, peaceful, warm, and happy to be home, she feels, to various degrees, frustrated, overworked, unappreciated, and unsupported. It is then extremely difficult for her to take time out for herself and appreciate life's simple pleasures.

When a woman feels overwhelmed at the end of the day, she is generally enough in touch with her female side to remember all her problems, but her male side demands that she find solutions and do something. In this state, it is hard for her to relax or even know what would nurture her female side.

When women are feeling overwhelmed, they are so focused on getting things done that they literally can't feel the inner needs and wants of their feminine sides. Each time they finish a task, rather than feel relieved, they begin to feel the inner emptiness and longing of their female sides.

Three Ways a Woman Goes Out of Balance

When a woman feels heavily overwhelmed, she doesn't feel safe talking in a non-goal-oriented manner because she has moved out of balance to her problem-solving male side and can't get back. This tends to manifest itself in three distinct ways.

Stage One: Feeling Overwhelmed and Overeating

A woman's most common reaction to undernourishment of her female side is to eat. Eating is an easy replacement for love. Through feeding herself, she can temporarily suppress the painful feelings of insecurity that are emerging from her female side. By numbing feelings, her potential for passion is stilled.

Women overeat to quench the deeper thirst for nurturing and secure relationships. This tendency is technically called a "need replacement." If she can't get what she really needs, the real need is replaced by another need that appears more attainable.

In this case, her need for love is replaced by her need for food. Until the craving for love is satisfied, she will always be hungry. Through eating more she is able to temporarily repress the persistent longings of her female side and find relief. In some cases, she may even fool herself temporarily into believing that she is quite happy and that she doesn't need to talk or share in a nurturing relationship.

Why Women Gain Weight

Quite commonly, soon after a woman gets married she frequently begins to put on weight in excess of the natural gain mandated by aging and childbirth.

This shift takes place not because the relationship has problems, but because marriage itself makes a woman relax and feel more secure. As her female side begins to blossom, it says "Now that I am loved, I can finally come out and be nurtured, supported, and heard." She begins involuntarily to experience emotions and urges that women have felt for centuries but which have been suppressed by modern independent living.

You see, as a woman connects more deeply with her female side, her natural tendency to talk about feelings and problems abruptly emerges. It is as if she is possessed by the spirits of her female ancestors. These alien feelings from her ancient past make her modern self feel that she is overly needy, emotional, illogical, petty, even weak. Many women are embarrassed by these feelings.

In a state of emotional confusion, the last thing a woman wants is to share the origins of that confusion with her spouse. In most cases, she doesn't even feel comfortable sharing these new feelings with other women. She doesn't know what to do because she never saw her mother successfully sharing feelings or problems with her father that resulted in her getting his respect and support. To avoid creating unnecessary conflict or frustrating her mate, she chooses to suppress the need to share these feelings coming from her female side and, as a result, feels a new need to eat more.

The more she eats, the more she is able to keep at bay these strange new feelings and tendencies, but only temporarily. Until she finds a way to fulfill and directly nurture her female side on a regular basis, she will continue to use food as a painkiller.

When a woman tries to solve the problem of overeating through dieting, she goes even farther out of balance by moving toward her male side. During a diet, the body feels the panic of famine and craves food even more. The female side is nurtured by feeling secure and supported. The imposition of strict discipline requiring control nurtures and strengthens the male side, not the female side.

Ease, comfort, effortlessness, security, fun, recreation, pleasure, and beauty all nurture the female side. Dieting does not. Recent diet programs that encourage women to *eat more* low-fat foods and exercise at a slow, easy pace instead of depriving themselves are definitely a better approach to losing weight. However, the most effective solution to female weight problems is more nurturing relationships and a less pressured, more relaxed lifestyle.

Stage Two: Women Who Do Too Much

When women are deprived of the support their female side requires to avoid feeling the pain of rejection, they move to their male side and begin exhibiting traditional masculine tendencies. They become increasingly goal oriented, competitive, assertive, independent, and efficient. They take great pride in being logical and rational. In most cases, life experiences or certain messages in childhood have conditioned them to reject feminine feelings as weak, undesirable, and unlovable.

It is hard for these women to see themselves as being lovable to men if they were to be soft and feminine. They work hard to hide their feminine sensitivities and needs. Incorrectly assuming that "femininity" is undesirable, they have no idea why a man would be attracted to "that."

These women deal with their inner female side by becoming hard instead of soft, tough instead of sensitive, and independent instead of dependent. Self-sufficiency is their primary method of coping. They tend to pull away from intimate conversation. In some cases, they even scorn the male support that could eventually bring them fulfillment and prevent them from shifting into the mode of doing more.

For some women, the tendency to "do more" means more domestic perfectionism. Everything has to be in its place, organized, and clean. For others, it simply implies that there is never enough time to relax. If women cannot relax because their male side demands solutions to their problems, passion quickly loses its magic and disappears, and sex becomes mechanical.

Other women do too much by taking on excessive responsibility. They have a hard time saying no when they feel needed. They may even feel compelled to do things that they are not even asked to do. They pride themselves on anticipating the needs of others and "being there" for them.

What a Man Can Do for Her

To support a woman, a man must understand that, deep inside, she longs to relax, let go, and surrender to someone she trusts to care for and support her. This is the true inner need of the female side.

However, because she judges her need for help as unacceptable, it is unconsciously replaced by a false need. The replacement need emerges as an urgent calling to fulfill others. She feels as if her happiness is based on providing fulfillment for others instead of getting her own needs satisfied. In a sense, she becomes the responsible and caring man she wishes could fulfill her.

This insight is valuable for both women and men. When a woman is becoming overly responsible, instead of chastising her for doing too much, a man can realize that she needs help in getting back to her feminine side. Without a supportive partner, women on their male side tend to become increasingly self-sufficient and thus decrease the possibilities of having a man support them.

Women who feel overwhelmed rarely get the support they need. They do not know how to be vulnerable or to ask for it. Since they are seen as self-sufficient, help is rarely offered. If it is, it's rejected. No one is allowed to see the vulnerable part of her. Everyone is encouraged to regard with admiration the strong and giving side.

Such women have trouble even contacting their needs and giving to themselves for a change. There is little a man can do for them unless he understands that the stronger these women appear, the more needy they are deep within.

Men without a deeper understanding are easily frustrated by women who do too much. The busier she is, the less time and appreciation she has for him. He does not feel that he can help her and then fulfill her.

No matter what he does for her, she is always driven to do more. On a feeling level, he feels cut off from her. If he cannot do for her, then he cannot receive her love. He doesn't feel that he can make a difference in her life. In a very real sense, her independence and sense of autonomy push him away.

These women do not understand that men love to make a difference; to be fulfilled a man needs to feel successful in providing for her fulfillment. This is how men experience greater intimacy with women.

How to Attract Mr. Right

Because it's more difficult for women who do too much to start relationships, they commonly ask me how to attract a man.

My response is to ask them why they *need* a man. The question invariably takes them by surprise. They give answers like:

"Well, I don't know if I really *need* a man" or "I'm not so sure that I *need* a man."

Others are more deliberate, clearly stating, "I don't really *need* a man, but I want one."

If these women are to secure a lasting relationship, they must first begin to open up to their feminine side, which feels no shame in saying "I need a man."

> **If women are to secure a lasting relationship, they must first begin to open up to their feminine side, which feels no shame in saying "I need a man."**

When a woman is in a hurry or desperate for a relationship, she is definitely feeling from her female side, but it's not sufficiently nurtured to attract the right man. Through nurturing her female side something magical begins to happen. She feels her need for a man and trusts that at the right time and in the right place she will find him. This openness can be cultivated by finding fulfillment in her female friendships without depending on a man, yet remaining open to receiving a man's support.

How Men Experience Intimacy

We must always keep in mind that a man bonds emotionally by successfully doing for a woman. A man experiences greater intimacy each time he succeeds in providing his partner with fulfillment. We must also remember that women experience greater intimacy primarily by receiving love and support. This is a very important distinction. If a woman *cannot* slow down and allow a man to nurture her female side, she will have trouble creating a bond in the first place.

A simple example of the new relationship skill of slowing down can be seen simply and graphically: a man and woman approach a door. Women who do too much will speed up, politely open the door, and wait for the man to walk through. They give to others what they need themselves, which only reinforces the tendency to give and not receive. To nurture her female side, a woman should practice slowing down to make sure he gets to the door first, waiting for him to open it, walking through, and thanking him. When she lets him open the door for her, she gives him an opportunity to support her successfully.

Rituals for Finding Balance

Through this dynamic, a man is placed in the masculine role of providing, and a woman moves to her feminine role of graciously receiving. It also clarifies her real need, which is to be cared for. She doesn't physically need him to open the door, but when he does, it supports and nurtures her female side. Her femininity needs and thrives on this kind of support in order to find balance.

When a man opens the door for a woman, it is as if he is saying "You are special to me, I care about you, I honor you, I am here for you, I understand you do so much for everyone so I am happy to help make things easier for you whenever I can."

This loving message is given each time a man goes a little out of his way to show consideration for making his partner's life easier and more comfortable. Actions speak much louder than words.

Stage Three: Women Who Want Men to Talk More

The third most common reaction women have when they experience the imbalance of emotional role reversal is to long for their men to talk more and share themselves in traditionally feminine ways.

A woman in this third stage longs for a man to open up and share his feelings the way she would if she were in balance. It is as though she wants him to be feminine before she can feel safe in being feminine.

These women fully believe that they would be fulfilled if their partners would only open up and be more sensitive and vulnerable.

> This longing for men to be softer and more sensitive
> is really a replacement need. It covers the women's
> real longing to be more sensitive and soft themselves.

Just as the overweight woman replaces her need for love with the need for food, or the woman who "does too much" replaces her need to be supported with the need to support others, this woman replaces her need to be feminine with the need for her partner to be feminine.

These replacement needs are not deliberate choices but are reflexive reactions that occur when women are required to function like men without the support they need to be feminine.

When a Woman Doesn't Feel Safe

A woman in a loving relationship may feel unsafe because she feels unlovable or because her partner hasn't yet learned how to make her feel secure. Regardless of why she doesn't feel safe, when she can't express her female side, she will automatically move to her male side and exhibit more masculine traits. To find balance, she will begin to crave a more "feminine" partner.

Generally, the man she chooses is already more sensitive and open. In some cases, though, he is originally a less sensitive man, but over time she tries to make him more feminine by demanding that he open up and share more or become more domestic. This reaction occurs because the woman doesn't have a clear picture of how to get the nurturing support she needs for her own female side. She feels driven to support his female side.

Instinctively she feels "If I can listen sympathetically to his problems and feelings, he'll listen to mine. If I can fulfill his feminine needs, he'll fulfill mine." While this formula works with other women, it does not work with men.

When a Woman Wants to Talk

I can tell when my wife really has something to tell me because she inevitably asks me lots of questions. For example, when I return from teaching my weekend seminars, she will sometimes be particularly interested in seeing me and asking lots of questions. This is a signal that she has a lot to share. I now understand that after answering a few questions, I am supposed to ask her questions about her weekend.

By cracking the secret feminine code, I have learned to give Bonnie what she's asking for. Before I understood how we were different, the same situation would turn into a major argument.

She would ask me questions about my weekend when she wanted to talk instead of simply telling me what she wanted to share. What I really wanted to do was relax quietly. But I could tell she wanted me to talk, so I would try. When I look back at those times, I can see that it was like pulling teeth. The more she wanted me to talk, the less I wanted to.

After a few minutes of answering her questions as briefly as possible, I felt as if I'd answered her questions (as a gift to her) and then would go relax and watch TV (as a gift for me). Little did I know that this was not what was expected. Now she was even more upset. Not only had I resisted her questions, I wasn't asking her questions in return.

The process only became positive when I could read the signals and begin applying new relationship skills. Now when Bonnie asks me lots of questions, I talk a little and then ask her lots of questions. If she is still not talking, I gently persist. Once she gets going, I let her do most of the talking because it is her need more than mine.

Never talking more than a woman as a general guideline counteracts the tendency to go into emotional role reversal. Certainly, on some occasions I will talk more, but when I begin to notice it is happening a lot, I pull back and focus on assisting her in opening up.

The startling truth that I have discovered only in the past ten years is that the more a woman is dependent on her partner to talk and open up, the farther she gets from her female side.

With this insight I eventually came to realize that the greatest gift I could give my clients was to help the men be successful in listening to the women. I would also help the women "prepare" them so that listening was not insurmountably difficult. Once a man eventually learned this skill, he didn't get so upset with his female partner's feelings. Suddenly, women were feeling much safer and freer about expressing their feelings. Using this approach, couples quite quickly felt more successful in their relationships.

How Women Begin to Feel When Men Open Up

Let's explore some of the diverse comments made by different women whose partners were more expressive of feelings than

He Does:	She Feels:
1. He shares how upset he feels when she talks about her feelings.	1. "I didn't realize he was so sensitive. Now I have to be careful all the time. I don't feel safe saying anything to him."
2. He becomes angry and shares his gut reactions to her feelings before taking time to cool off.	2. "No matter what I say, it's upsetting to him. I am afraid to open up with him."
3. He shares openly about all his problems in response to her talking about hers.	3. "He has enough problems. I don't want to burden him with mine. He is just too needy. I don't want another child."
4. He complains too much and always wants things to be better.	4. "I really appreciate that he's opened up, but now that I know him, I'm not really that attracted to him. I feel bad about it, but I really don't want to be with him anymore."
5. He shares his deep feelings of insecurity and his need to be loved.	5. "I care about his emotions, but I feel like I can't be me around him."
6. He talks too much about his feelings whenever he gets ticked off.	6. "I feel like I have to walk on eggshells when I am around him. I don't feel heard or understood."
7. He shares his hurt feelings and cries more than she does.	7. "I am embarrassed to say this, but when he cries all the time I can respect his feelings, but I lose all my romantic feelings for him."

He Does:	She Feels:
8. He gets angry a lot and feels that he has to get it out rather than silently contain his feelings in order to cool off.	8. "When he gets angry, I feel like he is a child throwing a tantrum. Automatically I begin to feel like I have to always please and mother him."
9. He talks about his problems more, or the problems with the relationship, than she does.	9. "I am really glad we are in therapy. He really needs it. I didn't realize he had so many problems. It's not that I'm perfect, I just feel like he needs someone else. I want to leave because I don't know what to do for him."
10. He whines and complains about things more than she does.	10. "I resent that he whines about everything. I want to be with a more masculine man. I don't want to be married to another woman."
11. He talks about his needs for more in the relationship and looks to his partner to fulfill his female side.	11. "He is always very attentive to me, but I feel that he is always needing more. When I don't talk, he gets upset, and when he talks, I just want to get out of the room. I listen, but I really don't want to."

they themselves were. While not every woman will relate to each of these, they are very common, particularly to women who have lived with men who are more sensitive.

None of these women could have predicted that they would feel this way. Like many women, they thought that if their male partner would just open up they would be in marital bliss.

How Women React to a Man's Sensitivities

The way a woman reacts to her partner's vulnerabilities is practically the opposite of how a man will respond to hers. If he hears her feelings *and doesn't feel blamed,* then he cares and connects with his own female side. By listening to a woman share, a man can feel sensitive to her feelings and yet strong and determined to help.

When a woman listens to a man's feelings, she also becomes stronger but resents having to care more for him when she needs him to care for her.

This shift in women can be extremely gradual and hard to detect. As a man opens up, she is initially very impressed and finds his behavior endearing. Unfortunately, she eventually tires of it and turns off to him. Even when she wants to leave him, she will feel that it is "not him but her." In many cases, however, it is because he opened up more than she did and she was simply turned off.

The bottom line here is that women are more fulfilled if their male partners reveal less but help them to reveal more.

> When a woman longs for a man to open
> up and be sensitive, she is really longing to
> open up and become more sensitive and
> vulnerable herself.

Three Ways a Man Goes Out of Balance

When a man doesn't feel appreciated in his relationship with a woman or at his job, he begins to shift out of balance in any of three ways.

Each of these reactions is counterproductive. They may bring immediate short-term relief from feeling the pain of not being supported on his male side, but in the long run they only weaken him more. They are addictive behaviors that assist him in avoiding his pain but do little to directly solve the real problem.

Stage One: Overworking

A man's most common impulse when he doesn't feel supported at home is to work harder at the office. As we have already discussed, a man reacts instinctively to a woman's dissatisfaction by trying to provide more money, so he becomes increasingly driven to achieve more and succeed more. No matter how successful he is, it is never enough. He silently criticizes himself for not being better, for making mistakes and not being good enough.

Through repeatedly focusing on his need for success (or his failure to achieve that success), he is temporarily freed from feeling his unfulfilled need to be appreciated by others. He avoids feeling unappreciated in his relationship by asserting his independence and competence at work.

He will convince himself that he doesn't need to be appreciated. This is only because he has not tasted the fulfillment of being appreciated for his every effort and action regardless of the result. Forgiveness, acceptance, and appreciation have not been his experience growing up or while in relationships with women.

In most cases, when a man begins drifting from a relationship focus to a work focus, he doesn't even know that he's missing the appreciation he used to get from his spouse. He may agree with her when she says, "Why should I appreciate him for emptying the trash, it's his trash too." Unaware that he needs to be appreciated for the little things, he seeks to do big things for her that should reap the reward of her favor. But they don't.

Without the daily experience of appreciation at home, a man begins to measure himself solely by the results of his work. Because his hunger for success is really a replacement for his true need to be appreciated, he is never satisfied with his success.

He is in a self-defeating pattern and is spiraling down. The more he focuses on work, the less he does directly for his wife. If he is not doing things directly for his wife, her appreciation will not touch him. Even if she does appreciate him, he can barely feel it. The less appreciated he feels, the more self-critical and dissatisfied he becomes.

This first stage inevitably leads him to the second stage of imbalance. When he comes home, he is unable to shift from the work mode to the relationship mode.

Stage Two: He Doesn't Come Out of His Cave

When a man comes home feeling unsuccessful at work, he immediately pulls away from his partner to relax and forget the problems of his day. As we have already discussed, temporarily pulling away is quite normal. However, since he is recovering from the added stress of feeling unsuccessful, it will take him much longer before he is ready to emerge.

But in stage two, he simply cannot forget the pressure. If a man feels bad about his work, it is much harder to feel good, even while pursuing a hobby or watching his favorite team. When the pressure to succeed predominates, the power of his cave time activities to release him from the grip of work diminishes proportionally.

When a man's male side is not sufficiently nurtured by his mate, he has little energy when he gets home. It is as if he is storing it up until he can confront his problems the next day. The masculine energy he used to bring to the relationship is greatly suppressed.

Men experience difficulties in forgetting work-related problems and pressures because their female side keeps reminding them of the problems, while their male side feels incapable of solving them. As a result, they become addicted to cave time activities in an attempt to forget the problems and pressures of work. Such men tend to be disinterested in what is going on around them.

It is hard for a man like this to connect with his partner because not only is he so preoccupied, he doesn't even have the motivation he once did. He has low energy because deep inside he feels like a failure.

Failure is deadly for a man.

A Man's Replacement Needs

In stage one, a man's replacement need is to succeed; in stage two, it is to rest and relax—even though his real need is to be loved and appreciated. He feels as though he wants to be ignored so that he can rest, nap, relax, or zone out by watching TV. While his "vegging out" is a legitimate need, his mate believes that he is just being lazy. That only makes it more difficult for him to hear or be responsive to her requests and needs.

Instead of being assertive, he becomes passive; instead of being interested, he is distracted; instead of wanting to connect, he wants to be left alone. Although resting will bring temporary relief, it does not satisfy his need to be energized by appreciation.

Without an understanding of what their mates require, women unknowingly make the situation worse. They complain that he is not there for them. They do not instinctively focus on appreciating what he does do for them. Even if a man does very little, a woman can still focus on what he *does* do instead of what he doesn't do. In this way, he will be assisted in eventually doing more and getting the appreciation he needs.

Once he gets going, it is like a snowball rolling down a hill, building up speed and growing bigger and bigger. As a man is appreciated for what he does, he will do a little more. When a man is appreciated, he will summon up the energy and motivation to do still more. With a woman's love, he can build up his strength to come out of the cave.

> **When a man is appreciated, he will summon up the energy and motivation to do still more.**

A woman can also help a man by helping herself. Her being happier will even help him to come out. When he sees that she isn't unhappy and blaming him for not coming out, he feels he must be doing something right.

When a woman is happy, a man tends to take the credit and feel good about himself. For example, if he supports her financially, if she goes shopping and returns thanking him for what he bought, he'll feel much better.

The downside of a man's taking the credit for a woman's feelings is that when she is not happy, he feels that he's more of a failure and retreats even deeper into his cave.

When men are in this stage, women tend to criticize them for being lazy and unsupportive. By understanding this second stage, it will be much more possible for her to be compassionate and supportive instead of nagging and complaining.

Comparing Men and Women

By comparing a man's second stage to her own, a woman can increase her understanding. Just as it is difficult for a woman to move out of stage two, it is equally difficult for a man.

A woman in the second stage feels compelled to do more.

For her to relax and slow down, she needs a lot of support. When she is married or has children, she is even more driven. Almost every woman knows how hard it is to relax and have a good time when feeling overwhelmed and needed by others.

In a similar but opposite way, a second-stage man feels driven to do less. He can easily relax but cannot feel motivated to do more. He is energized by the thought of some recreational activity but becomes suddenly exhausted by the thought of being domestically responsible. He feels a strong need to rest, and do less, while she feels a strong need to do more. Just as she can't do something fun and for herself, that is all he has the energy to do.

Without understanding this dynamic, a relationship can just make it worse for the man. The more he is needed, the more disappointed others who depend on him will be. As a result, he becomes even more immobilized.

With this knowledge, a woman can begin to imagine what her man is going through. In a similar way, men can fathom why women in stage-two imbalance can't just "relax and take it easy."

Moving the Couch Potato

Understanding stage two of emotional role reversal has helped me immensely. At times when I am not feeling good about my work, I tend to stay in my cave for extended periods of time. Even though I would like to come out, I feel trapped.

To get myself out, I remember that what I really need is appreciation. My body is telling me that I need to rest and relax, but my mind now knows better.

So I force myself up off the couch even though every cell in my body is saying rest, relax, don't get up. I imagine I am lifting weights to build up my muscles. When I am out of shape, lifting weights is always a strain and I don't want to do it. But once I do, I feel much better and stronger.

In a similar way, when I am feeling like a couch potato and I am glued to the couch, I lift myself up and do something physically that I know my wife will appreciate. It can be as basic as getting up to empty the trash. Once I start moving, she can give me some appreciation. Soon my engines start pumping again.

This technique works especially well because Bonnie takes pains to appreciate my effort. When I do something at home, instead of reacting like "So what, I've been busy since I got home," she will take a moment to articulate her gratitude.

If she doesn't notice what I do, instead of missing an opportunity to be appreciated I can say, "Did you notice that I emptied the trash?"

In response, she will always take a moment to say, "Oh, thanks."

Even if she is resenting me and her guts are saying "Big deal," she makes a point of saying something brief but nice.

Knowing that I can easily be appreciated in my relationship helps me tremendously in coming out of my cave. The repeated experience of appreciation allows me to feel my need for it and then come out and get it. The certain anticipation of her warm responses always helps motivate me to get out of my cave.

If Bonnie takes the time to appreciate me when she is in stage two, it helps her as well. By appreciating me, she is taking a moment to become aware that she really isn't alone and that she does have my support. So she begins to relax. For example, when I come out of my cave to empty the trash, she is not just appreciating me for emptying the trash, she is appreciating me for being her companion, friend, and partner in life.

Her support frees me from getting trapped in my cave. This does not mean that I don't take cave time. When a man is stressed, it is healthy and natural for him to go to his cave. It only becomes unhealthy when he can't come out again.

Relationships and the Cave

When a man is single, there is nothing preventing him from coming out of his cave whenever he feels like it. When he is in a relationship, however, it is nearly impossible for him to come out if his mate resents his pulling away, and sits waiting at the door. Too many women unknowingly make this mistake and actually end up working against their own desires.

When a man is in the cave, a woman wants more from him but can sense that if she asks he will resist like a grumbling bear. It doesn't occur to her that like a bear he is hungry for the honey of her love. She believes that if he talks about his feelings, he'll feel better. Needless to say, the more she tries to get him out by suggesting he do things or by asking him questions, the more he resists.

How to Get a Bear out of His Cave

With this new awareness, she can use the new relationship skills that her mother never knew to get him out. She can do it by pretending that he literally is a bear.

No one in their right mind would enter a bear's cave while he was sleeping, nor would they try to pull him out.

Instead, you would indirectly draw him out by leaving little pieces of bread outside his door. If the bread doesn't work, you put honey on it. When he smells it, his instincts will tell him to follow the scent. He appears.

Now you begin to sense that he will go wherever you want him to if you leave a trail of bread and honey behind you. If the "bear" is a human male, the bread is the opportunity to do something, and the honey is the appreciation he will get by doing it. Men, like bears, are looking for honey. When they clearly smell acceptance and appreciation, they are motivated to leave the cave.

Stage Three: He Wants More Support from Her

When a man's male side is not supported and he feels stuck in the cave, a third reaction occurs. His male side stays in the cave, but his female side comes out. Suddenly, he wants his partner to take care of him, but because he is still a man, he demands it in an aggressive way.

We know that when a man is in his cave, a woman should not try to go in after him. In third-stage imbalance, he comes out all right—but with all guns blazing. He is easily hurt, offended, and provoked.

Like a woman, he feels he is "doing everything" and not getting nearly enough back. He has moved way over on his female side and is generally very verbally expressive.

Whenever a man cannot fully come out of his cave, his female side tends to emerge and take control of the relationship. He will tend to overreact to his mate's mistakes, feel a much greater need to talk about his feelings, become much more defensive of his actions, and will demand apologies when she has upset him.

The Need to Be Respected

In this stage of emotional role reversal, a man's real need is still to be appreciated, but because he is not getting the kind of support he really requires, a replacement need takes over. The true need to be appreciated is replaced by the need to be respected.

A man in this third stage will from time to time present these kinds of demands. When he does, the most effective steps he can take to stop himself are to cease talking to his partner about his feelings and set about containing them. Talking only makes him more rigid, righteous, demanding, and punishing. These are examples of remarks that indicate that a man must get a grip on himself.

What Happens:	His Gut Reactions in Stage Three:
1. She expresses feelings of frustration or disappointment.	1. "If you can't be happy, then we should just end this relationship."
2. She expresses unsolicited advice.	2. "You know I don't like it when you talk to me that way. Don't do it."
3. She expresses disapproval about something he did or forgot to do.	3. "No one can treat me this way. If you do not change, then I will leave you."
4. She is in a bad mood and unable to be appreciative.	4. "I do everything for you and this is what I get in return."
5. She complains about something he hasn't done.	5. "How dare you treat me this way. I will not stand for it. You are so ungrateful."
6. She disapproves of something he did and gives advice.	6. "I will not put up with this anymore. I do everything right, and you are wrong."
7. They get into a heated argument over something petty.	7. "I just can't stand this anymore. I don't deserve to be treated like this. You will never learn. That's it, I'm finished."
8. She does something to annoy him.	8. "I don't want to be mean, but you make me this way. I have to teach you a lesson."

While the above expressions may accurately reflect what he's feeling, it is lethal to express them to his mate. They are entirely negative, selfish, arrogant, shaming, and controlling and can do nothing to create a climate of trust and openness. If he is at all interested in getting the love and support he truly needs, then he must practice containing these kinds of feelings. Yes, they are his gut reactions but not the reactions of his heart and mind. Before he talks, he should first be centered in his heart and mind, not his guts.

A man in emotional role reversal has gone respect crazy. When he gets through making others feel guilty or intimidated, he is only temporarily satisfied. His hunger for respect will grow because his soul is really asking for appreciation. Whenever there is a problem, he has to be right and he is quick to blame and reject others.

In the third stage, a man may want more communication. He demands to know his woman's feelings, yet when she tells him, he argues and wants to share more of his own. Although he is acting like a woman in needing to share, he is still a man and generally wants to be right and is very willing to argue.

These spirited arguments feel good to him but bring only temporary relief. He will continue to feel a strong need to be heard and obeyed. No matter what a woman does for him, it will never be enough.

When Men Get Angry

The difference between men in this stage and a woman who needs to be heard is that when a man feels the strong need to share his feelings he will also want to be right. When a woman needs to share feelings, generally speaking she only requires that she feel heard and validated. She does not require a man to agree with her.

This third stage is greatly encouraged by popular culture. In the last twenty years, men are repeatedly encouraged to get in touch with feelings and to express them. In many cases, they are shamed for not being more expressive of their feelings.

As we have already noted, when a man expresses too many

sensitivities, a woman tires of him. Particularly when a man expresses anger, a woman begins to close up. Because she doesn't feel safe in sharing with him, she refuses to talk. Suddenly *she* is in her cave and *he* is trying to get in.

When a Woman Won't Talk

At my seminar, men in the third stage generally share similar complaints. Let's explore a common example.

Tim was very angry when he stood up to share his story. He complained that he was much more willing to work on the relationship than his wife.

"You say women want to talk," he grumbled. "I want to talk more, but my wife won't talk to me."

The righteous tone in his voice tipped me off to what was wrong. "Has your wife ever said to you that you don't listen and that she can't talk to you?" I asked him.

"Sure. That's all she'll say," he answered. "But it's not true. I will listen. I am the one who wants to talk more. I do all the things you say a man should do. I cook, clean, make dates, and do all the things women are supposed to want, and then she spends all her time in the cave. I have had it."

"Well, that's the reason she won't talk to you. You don't listen," I told him flatly.

He then proceeded to prove my point by arguing with me: "No, you don't understand. I do listen, I am supportive, I listen to her feelings, but I also expect her to listen to mine."

"The way you are talking to me is probably just the way you talk to her," I persisted. "By arguing, you are ensuring that she will not want to talk with you. Even if she was warming up to the idea of sharing with you, your approach would stop her dead in her tracks."

A woman simply cannot feel protected or respected when a man speaks to her in such a righteous and demanding tone, particularly when it comes to talking about her feelings.

When a man is too emotionally demanding or overly sensitive and easily hurt, a woman feels as if she can't trust him to hear her feelings correctly.

She will not feel safe opening up with him when he feels he needs to talk more than she does. The only recourse left open to her is going to her cave.

This means moving more to her male side, because to protect herself from her partner's emotionally charged attacks and demands, she has to become like a man. After a while she will feel so comfortable in her cave that her female side will *want* to stay there.

Why a Man Gets So Upset

When a man is on his female side, it will sound very unfair to him when his partner won't talk to him or apologize for upsetting him. He feels powerless to get what he needs unless she agrees with him and expresses a willingness to change. He does not know how naturally women change when they feel loved.

When a woman feels loved, she slowly begins to open up and is willing to change unsupportive behaviors. When her mate is demanding, she will inevitably resist him, which of course only makes him feel angrier and more demanding.

When a stage-three man is upset, he is basically feeling deprived of the support he wants and deserves. To feel better, he needs an effective game plan for getting what he wants.

When a man comes up with a workable solution that makes sense to him, he begins to move back to his masculine side, which wants to solve the problem.

When a woman doesn't want to talk and a man does for healthy reasons, this is what he can do:

He should say: "I can tell something is bothering you. What's wrong?"

He should not say: "I am upset and I need to talk with you."

She says: "I can't talk to you."

He should say: "Hmmm," and then just pause and consider how he probably gives the message that it's not safe for her to talk.

He should not say: "Of course you can talk to me. I am the one who is trying to get you to talk. I am the one who is trying to make this relationship work."

If she says: "You will just argue with me. I don't want to even get started."

He should say: "You're probably right."

What is most important is that he should remain calm and accepting. This is the only way to win his partner over. He needs to prove to her that he can duck and dodge her provocations without getting mad. With this kind of safety insurance, she will begin to open up.

He should not say: "I will not argue, I just want to talk!" That would be arguing.

To argue with a woman when she doesn't want to talk just confirms that she can't open up and talk to him. To make it safe for a woman to open up and be feminine in a relationship, he must practice containment. He should contain his feelings so that she can first feel heard.

This does not mean that he should never feel or express his feelings. It means that he shouldn't overwhelm her with more negative feelings than she can handle. Instead of spilling his guts, he should go to his cave and think. After he has calmed down, he should focus on the solution, not the problem. He should come up with a workable strategy for doing something that will get him the appreciation he really craves.

When Men Make Lists

I can tell I'm in stage three of emotional role reversal when my female side comes out and starts making lists of all the things my partner is doing wrong. When I start making lists, unlike a woman who primarily just needs to talk about her lists, I want Bonnie to agree with me and promise to correct her behavior.

When I used to express myself in this way, Bonnie felt that she was living with a domineering tyrant. It was the "me" I become when I am not able to be my true loving self. The domineering tyrant is my shadow self.

If we are not feeling loved, we become the opposite of who we are when we are wonderful and loving. People who are very generous become very tight when their gifts are not appreciated. People who are very trusting and open become completely closed when they feel disappointed. When people who are very patient and flexible finally reach their limit, they become impatient and rigid. This is how love turns to hate. As a man or a woman moves into emotional role reversal, their shadow selves make more and more appearances.

> **If we are not feeling loved, we become the opposite of who we are when we are wonderful and loving.**

To create and preserve a loving relationship, we need lots of ways in which to help us keep our balance, particularly when strong winds blow and the earth shakes beneath our feet.

For example, I still sometimes feel like a tyrant, but I do my best to keep these feelings to myself. I recognize at these moments that my male and female sides are imbalanced and do something to recover my equilibrium. Instead of acting out, I go to my cave. From inside my cave, I wait till I want to feel better. Then, to come out, I do something that will ensure my getting the appreciation from Bonnie that I really need in order to feel better. Instead of complaining that I am not appreciated, I do things that will garner her appreciation.

Through the application of new relationship skills the pitfalls and dangers of emotional role reversal can be gradually overcome. We will explore more ways in which men and women can find balance. We will also explore how to sustain the passion in a marriage through maintaining balance and being monogamous. We will explore the secrets of lasting passion to create a lifetime of love.